CBS

D0597212

WITHDRAWN

LITERARY MONOGRAPHS · Volume 9
Measuring Old English Rhythm

Literary Monographs Editorial Board

ROBERT S. BAKER

SARGENT BUSH, JR.

BARTON R. FRIEDMAN

RICHARD N. RINGLER

ERIC ROTHSTEIN, *Editor*

ANDREW D. WEINER

8088
L712
v.9

LITERARY
MONOGRAPHS

EDITED BY
Eric Rothstein

Volume 9

Measuring Old English Rhythm:
An Application of the Principles of Gregorian
Chant Rhythm to the Meter of Beowulf

Jane-Marie Luecke, O.S.B.

Published for the Department of English by

THE UNIVERSITY OF WISCONSIN PRESS

Published 1978
The University of Wisconsin Press
Box 1379, Madison, Wisconsin 53701
The University of Wisconsin Press, Ltd.
70 Great Russell Street, London

Copyright © 1978
The Board of Regents of the University of Wisconsin System
All rights reserved

First printing

Printed in the United States of America

ISBN 0-299-07510-9; LC 66-25869

Publication of this volume has been made possible in part
by a gift to the University of Wisconsin Foundation from
the estate of Beatrice T. Conrad, Davenport, Iowa

PREFACE

The Department of English of the University of Wisconsin continues with this volume a series of monographs in English and American literature. The series was inaugurated in 1967 to serve scholars whose work might take a form too lengthy for journals but too brief for a separate book.

The editorial board of *Literary Monographs* would like to express its appreciation to the University of Wisconsin Foundation for making possible the publication of this volume through a gift from the estate of Beatrice T. Conrad, Davenport, Iowa.

Eric Rothstein

Madison, Wisconsin
January 1978

CAT Feb 13'79

12-05-78   B-b   14.56

78-4218

CONTENTS

MEASURING OLD ENGLISH RHYTHM:
AN APPLICATION OF THE PRINCIPLES
OF GREGORIAN CHANT RHYTHM
TO THE METER OF *BEOWULF*

INTRODUCTION

For more than twenty-five years Old English scholars have been making specific references to the likeness they perceive between the rhythm of OE poetry and that of Gregorian Chant. None of these scholars has set about to demonstrate *how* it is like Gregorian Chant; hence, more than a dozen years ago I did just that in a dissertation that I sanguinely thought at the time would end the speculation.[1]

However, that work remained mostly unpublished (though copyrighted) because I initially turned my attention to applying the principles I had learned from it to rewriting Gregorian Chant melodies to fit the rhythm of the English texts in post-Vatican II liturgies.[2] It probably remained unpublished also because the articles and first drafts of this book, written in the late sixties, still used the terminology of structural linguistics, which at the time fit so admirably the concepts in the scholarship on Gregorian Chant rhythm. Publishers' delays and financial crises have made my work that has appeared[3] something of an anachronism in a prosodic world of transformational and generative rule. Hence, it was still possible for Thomas Cable in 1974 to list only three critics—Baum, Bliss, and Taglicht—as having made reference to Gregorian Chant in relation to OE poetry.[4]

Cable's volume, *The Meter and Melody of Beowulf* (which incorporates three articles that had appeared during the previous five years), seems to me one of the more significant contributions to OE prosody during the last decade, not because of an original thesis (although there are original contributions in it) but because it has reestablished some essential statements about OE meter. One of these, I think, finally put to rest all of the fallacies inherent in Bliss's 1358 "light verses"[5] by reasserting that there are always two metrical stresses in an OE verse regardless of their linguistic intensity. The other is a readoption of the four member theory of Kaluza—four members in a verse but not related to isochronous tim-

1

ing—which is also implicit in the theory of John Collins Pope, who makes the members fit into musical bars of equal time.[6]

As a result of Cable's book, which was being written at approximately the same time this manuscript was first prepared, I have completely revised my text in order to use Cable's work where it supports mine, to eliminate my weaker evidence where Cable's is stronger, and to oppose his arguments where my evidence makes them doubtful. The result is a better work, of course, especially since in the revision process I could easily divest myself of allegiance to any specific school of linguistics, use terminology more generally prosodic, and maintain more specifically the relation between my measurement of OE verses and the measurement theory of Gregorian Chant rhythm.

And that is, after all, the chief aim of this study—to show *how* the rhythm of *Beowulf* is *like* the rhythm of Gregorian Chant. I do this by applying very systematically a process of measuring into binary and ternary groups all the rhythmical material (linguistic syllables and boundaries) in a phrasal verse in exactly the same way that the Gregorian Chant masters measure their rhythmical (melodic and linguistic) material. This procedure deals with the rhythm, as distinct from the meter, of a single work, *Beowulf,* and its wider objective is to show the rhythmical variations that an OE scop could employ within the framework of OE meter.

Although it is not the aim, here, to develop a theory of OE meter, nevertheless a great deal is said or implied or, perhaps more accurately, first *assumed* and then *revealed* about that meter. The assumption is, first of all, that meter is the abstract pattern or scheme of a given poem or tradition of poetry, which is descriptive of its practice, rather than generative and determinative of its potential.[7] Thus, I *assume* in my study that the basic meter in OE poetry is a pattern of four members having two phrase stresses and making up a short, phrasal line-unit called a verse, and that in OE practice two of these verses were linked into long lines by alliterating some of the phrase stresses. My measurement of the OE rhythmical material in the concrete realization of this meter supports this assumption, because it demonstrates how the pattern is maintained even when the rhythmical material is so varied as to obscure and *all but* eliminate it for all auditory purposes.

The *all but* is an important qualification. It is the poet's intention always to generate a tension between his "given" meter and the rhythmical variations he creates within that meter. The aim of the prosodist, similarly, once she accepts a given meter as a working hypothesis, is to discover the toleration threshold, so to speak, for rhythmical variation within that meter. And it is also this aim that my measurement of *Beowulf* according to the system devised for measuring Gregorian Chant rhythm seems to serve.

Very briefly, the measurement shows that the four members of an OE verse may be single syllables or whole measures including boundary pulses, thus allowing for a variation in length from four pulses to as many as twelve; that the two phrase stresses of the meter may create not five but six types or patterns; that the poet could allow material around the line breaks between verses to be either necessary to the basic pattern or extraneous to it; and finally that the irregular principle of a free mixing of twos and threes (in binary and ternary measures, in verses of two and three and four measures, in alliterating patterns of two or three or double-crossed four) may have allowed the poet to use a rare single-verse line or three-verse long line. Whether all of these variations (which the demonstration seems to describe as possible within the meter) were considered successful poetry is a question that cannot be answered in this kind of study. Rather it is their description that is my study's second aim, as well as something of its fruit. But, once again, my primary aim is simply to demonstrate *how* the rhythm of *Beowulf* is like that of Gregorian Chant. If the principle of rhythm in both has the same origin in the irregular grouping of sounds in movement, first into small (nonisochronous) units and then into rhythmic syntheses, then my work may show *how* that principle is explained by Gregorian Chant masters and *how* it applies—if it does apply—to the verses of *Beowulf*.

1 SURVEYING THE HISTORY OF OLD ENGLISH PROSODY

*I*t was possible in the early 1960s to group OE prosodists in two categories: the timers and the stressers; or to use other terms designating the same dichotomy: the musical scanners and the stress-pattern scanners. Because of the influence of the major proponents of each category, one usually referred to them as the school of Pope and the school of Sievers. However a third group, at first superficially considered to be part of the Sievers school because of its concern for language patterns, was then gaining momentum and believed capable of resolving the opposition. This group, although originally structural linguists, will probably be recognized historically by the names of the generative linguists Halle and Keyser, whose theory created a circle, or school, of supportive and successive theories.

Today, then, we can speak of three schools in the history of OE prosody, the timers, the stressers, and the linguists,[1] as having contributed to an understanding of the metered rhythm found in the lines of *Beowulf.* Because each of the schools left something unaccounted for in its careful exposition of the aspect of meter or rhythm which was its major concern, there have also been groups of demurrers, who essentially attempted to devise systems for reconciling aspects of the diverging schools. The latest voice among these is Thomas Cable, whose work provides the immediate background to this volume.[2]

THE SCHOOL OF POPE: EQUAL TIMERS

Language is sound; hence, it occurs in time. And when like elements in the sounds are recognized as recurring, they tend to take on a life of their own—an aspect of their music is heard over their meaning. Music in this connection is directly related to intervals of time, and this has historically been assumed to mean equal intervals, an isochronous movement. This assumption came from two sources: first, the nature of the abstract meter with either two regularly recurring stresses or four recurring members, or both, in successive half-lines tends to impose an isochronous regularity on the linguistic material; and secondly, Western music theory from the seventeenth to the twentieth centuries has assumed that music always falls into equal measures of time.

The timers were the first to analyze Old Germanic and OE poetry. As early as 1705, George Hickes in working on OE verse had been concerned with the temporal basis of feet, *"quorum tempora aliquam ad se invicem habent rationem seu aptam proportionem, ex diversorum temporum vel motuum concinna & convenienti mensura compositam."*[3] But no one followed Hickes in OE or an analogous poetry (i.e., using the alliterative line) until Lachmann, working on the *Hildebrandslied,* announced the four-beat theory in 1833.[4] Most of the men who followed Lachmann were working on Old High German fragments, but in 1861 Müllenhoff applied the four-beat theory to OE, and in 1870 Schubert, in his dissertation "De Anglosaxonum arte metrica" treated the verse of *Beowulf* and of the *Genesis* in detail.[5]

This original four-beat theory provided for elasticity in the meter, since the two primary stresses could occur on any two of the four beats while the four beats maintained the isochronous timing. However, these early theorists did distinguish between stronger and weaker *Hebungen,* and it was this distinction that accounted for the two-beat theory of Wackernagel (1848), Reiger (1864), and Vetter (1872). Sievers' system of Five Types,[6] first introduced in 1885, actually followed from the two-beat theory, but its wide reception forced the timers to oppose it and thus to become more detailed. Hence, Möller in 1888 used musical bar lines in an attempt to prove that the primary stresses (*Haupthebungen*) occurred in equal intervals of time.[7]

The full significance of this reaction and its consequences in the history of OE prosody is not readily apparent. Sievers' attention to patterns of stress and unstress (*Hebung und Senkung*) caused the scholars concerned with timing to form an opposing school, and hence to become defensive. Less discernible as a consequence are the two lines of development that followed within the school of equal timers itself. One tradition follows from the old four-beat theory which used four little measures to stabilize the timing across the half-line; the other follows from Möller and the two-beat theory which used musical bar lines in two measures to equalize the intervals between the two strong stresses. The two lines have come down to the present day in the work of John Collins Pope and John Nist.[8]

John Nist seems to me to be the best current reader in the two-beat tradition. I say this because he begins his pattern (S O L O S O L O) always with the first primary stress, and describes this half-line pattern as forming a cadence "extending from the first primary stress of a half-line to the last syllable of its second measure" (p. 102). Hence, syllables preceding this first primary stress (such as occur in all verses of B and C types) are "extracadential," and the time between the two primary stresses (each of which begins a measure) is equalized.[9]

Nist's rule, which demands that the two primary stresses begin the two measures, is the essential characteristic of this line of development. Möller began with the original Germanic and based his theory on the assumption that before the accent became fixed on the root syllable, and before inflections began to be lost, the original Germanic half-line consisted of four bars of $\frac{2}{4}$ time, with or without anacrusis:

$$(x) \mid \text{x́x} \mid \text{x́x} \mid \text{x́x} \mid \text{x́x} \parallel \text{x́x} \mid \text{x́x} \mid \text{x́x} \mid \text{x́x} \mid$$
$$ 12 \quad\; 12 \quad\; 12 \quad\; 12 \quad\; 12 \quad\; 12 \quad\; 12 \quad\; 12$$

But later (and in OE) when the Germanic accent became fixed on the root syllable, giving the first syllable of polysyllabic words greater stress, the bar divisions changed to two bars of $\frac{4}{4}$ time, with secondary accents on the third beats:

$$(x) \mid \text{x́xx̀x} \mid \text{x́xx̀x} \parallel \text{etc.}$$
$$ 1234 \quad\; 1234$$

In later Germanic poetry such as OE, the loss of inflectional endings in the language prevented these measures from being ideally filled.

Möller did two things to overcome the resulting difficulty in scansion: he granted pauses or rests when *Moren* are missing; and he said that one long syllable may be used in place of two short ones (x x). On these assumptions he classified measures as *voll* (full: x́ x x̀ x), *klingend* (feminine: x́ x x̀), or *stumpf* (masculine: x́ x), obtaining nine different types of alliterative half-lines depending on the combination of two measures or bars in a half-line. When unstressed syllables occurred before the first primary stress, they were not included in the two measures. Three examples are sufficient to illustrate the types:

```
         x́  x   x̀  r       x́  x   x̀  x
204a: hwét tòn   |  hýge-ròfne          (a klingend + a voll)


         x      x́  x  r r    x́    x
1b:  in  |  géar--  |  dágum            (two stumpf with anacrusis)


       x́x  x̀ r      x́x  x̀
16a: lánge      hwí l è                 (two klingend)
```

Heusler's theory, which appeared in 1925 in the first volume of *Deutsche Versgeschichte,* follows most clearly from Möller: (1) each half-line contains two syllables that may carry primary stress; (2) each measure begins with one of these two stressed syllables; (3) there is normally a syllable bearing secondary stress in the middle of each measure, although this may be filled by a rest or by sustaining the preceding syllable; (4) the number of additional syllables between the two stress points is variable, depending on how many can be spoken in the time allotted to the measure; and (5) the unstressed syllables before the first stress are extrametrical, although they can in some instances be included temporally in the preceding half-line.[10]

Heusler devised the following signs to represent musical values: -, x, ⌣, ∧, for half note, quarter note, eighth note, and quarter rest, respectively. Klaeber, in his third edition of *Beowulf and the Fight at Finnsburg,* included specimens of Heusler's scansion of *Beowulf* using these signs, but Pope reprinted the lines with the symbols translated into musical notation. The following three examples include all five of Sievers' types and illustrate all the points of Heusler's theory:

193: (A) nȳdwracu   niþgrim   (E) nihtbealwa   mæst

26: (B) him ðā   Scyld gewāt   (C) tō gescæphwīle

164: (C) swā fela   fyrena   (D) fēond mancynnes

If one translates the symbols Nist has devised for his theory into musical notation, the line of development from Heusler is most readily apparent, although there are some real differences also. For example, Nist makes much more of the necessity for four accents in the half-line, with a resulting overemphasis that he considers characteristic of the Germanic tradition. It seems to me that the use of the P, which I have transcribed as a rest, makes this apparent as a quarter note would not:

```
        SP  LP    SP  L  P
11a: gomban  gyldan
```

```
          S  P  L  O     S  P  LP
649b: niht  ofer  ealle
```

This four-stress half-line, which would seem to put Nist in the line of development from the four-beat theory, does not, however, because of his principle that the two measures begin with the first primary stress, thus forcing the preceding unstressed syllables in all B and C type half-lines again to be extra-metrical.

```
        SP  L   O    S    O   L   O      L   O  SPLP    SPLP
1163: gan  under  gyldnum  beage, ‖ þær  þa  godan  twegen
```

Nist made much of the use of the harp; but since Pope had already introduced the idea of a harp stroke to fill in an initial rest some fifteen years earlier, Nist's contribution lies largely in his increased use of the instrument, particularly in its substitution for missing secondary stresses in his four-beat, but two-measure, dipodic rhythm, as in the following:

```
        SH   S  P  L  O
742a: bat  ban-locan
```

```
          S  O  L    O    S  H
93a: wlite-beorhtne  wang
```

Translating the symbols of Heusler and Nist into musical notation is actually misleading and does an injustice to both men. However, since Pope uses musical notation, and since his theory is probably known to every OE scholar, the use of notation makes comparison easier. Nevertheless, it should be emphasized that those prosodists who do not use such notation have probably made this choice for a significant reason: the notation gives an impression of rigid timing (of metronomic isochroneity) which they do not wish to emphasize.

The other line of development, from the original four-beat theory, includes some important names (ten Brink, Trautmann, Kaluza, Leonard, and Pope) and a number of minor ones.[11] The characteristic that distinguishes this line from the preceding one is its use of four little measures, by which the lesser-stressed syllables preceding the first primary stress in verses of types B and C are included in the measurement since the two primary stresses may fall in any of the four measures.

Ten Brink's theory preceded the use of the bar line and assumed that the typical or "ideal" line is iambic, deriving from a primitive Germanic line such as this:

x x́ x x́ x x́ x x́ ‖ x x́ x x́ x x́ x x́

which would have become in Old English:

    x) x̆   x x́   x   x̆   x x́
505a: ge hedde un der heofenum ‖ etc.

The theorists who followed him made each stress into a duple measure, thus producing four bars of $\frac{2}{4}$ time in a half-line. Trautmann used such a fundamental scheme as follows:

    x́ ⌣ | ⌣ ⌣ | ⌣ ⌣ | ⌣ ⌣
    ofer   heofo-   na ge-   hl i du

and he evolved sixteen subdivisions and twelve further subforms by contracting any two *Weilen* of a bar into one long syllable, as in the following:

    x́   ⌣ | ⸗ | ⌣ ⌣ | ⸗
  7b: h ē þæs fro-fre ge-bad

    ⸗ | ⸗ | ⸗ | ⸗
 16a: l an- ge   hw ī - l e

Max Kaluza criticized Trautmann's system because of its concern to fill the four little measures. His own aim was to show how the various speech material found in Sievers' Five Types might be reconciled with the four-beat theory. In his concern then for the rhythmic grouping of speech material, Kaluza tried to avoid the term "beats" and spoke of half-lines having four "members," and later he avoided the use of the word "bar" as wrongly producing a concept of time. He also used rests to fill gaps in the four members and introduced the concept of an initial rest at the beginning of a half-line, thus anticipating Pope by almost forty years.[12] However, it seems to me that Kaluza moved away from a consistent theory of four isochronous members, especially in his handling of B and C type verses.[13]

Like Kaluza, other men early in this century, influenced particularly by Sievers' system of the Five Types, made efforts to recognize the natural rhythm of speech material and still bring it within the bounds of equal

time. This was true especially in this country, where the influence of
Sidney Lanier was so strong as to prompt one writer to demand that
prosodists scotch their "false start" in Anglo-Saxon metrics and "return to
the rock foundation of Lanier." [14] Inevitably, the effort to unite the two
schools gave rise to ambiguous statements by the theorists. For example,
Edwin B. Setzler very early in the century insisted on "the co-ordination of
the sounds into equal time-groups" because the "very nature of rhythm
requires . . . at least *approximately* equal intervals of time." Setzler used
Sievers' types throughout, fitting them into the required "equal-time"
measures, insisting that "after the type of rhythm has been definitely
established . . . the number of sounds that comprise any individual foot
may be varied at pleasure within certain limits, and . . . rests and pauses
may be used to complete the normal time of the measure." [15]

The ambiguity can probably be traced to rather too-simplistic assumptions and to a careless use of such terms as "musical." For example, James
Routh, in a theory that is an interesting variation and extension of
Setzler's, assumed that the "five-type meters were themselves spontaneous
and musical devices" and stated that they must therefore "conform to
musical law." [16] According to Routh, and apparently to all the musical
scanners, "the only known musical law of rhythm is a beating of time."
Routh's own theory says that all the Sievers-types reduce to five members
(rather than four): x'x'x (where the x's stand for a variable number of
unstressed syllables or a pause). By displacing an unstressed syllable by a
pause in one position, he achieves types A, C, and B. By displacing it in
two positions and reducing the secondary stress to an additional unstressed syllable, he achieves types D and E, as follows:

        A: ∧′x′x
        C: x′∧′x
        B: x′x′∧
        D: ∧′∧′xx
        E: ∧′xx′∧

It was William Ellery Leonard who really believed in what Kaluza
called *"die gute, alte, viel geschmaehte und oft todtgesagte, aber deshalb nur
um so zaeher am leben festhaltende Lachmannsche vierhebungstheorie"* and
who restored the four-beat theory.[17] Leonard's work with the *Niebelungen*
and other Old Germanic poetry reinforced his contention that the four
beats, even the weakest of them, "mark time in the verse, which Sievers'
unaccented syllables don't." In 1929[18] he went much further in developing
the idea of the rest (as occurring between the beats) and rest-beat (as a
substitute for a beat on a syllable) as organic phenomena in early OE, ON,

and so on, and emphasized that "the time is kept either by unstressed speech-material or by a rest."

Leonard added to his 1929 article a footnote in which he admits to an affinity with Andreas Heusler's theory. It may have been such an admission that misled Pope in 1942 into overlooking some of the contributions of both Leonard and Kaluza and into concentrating on Heusler, whose theory he described as second best only to his own (p. 20). By his elaborate presentation of Heusler's readings, he makes his own theory appear to resolve the problems left unsolved by Heusler. With reference to the numbered list of the tenets of Heusler's theory given on page 7 above, Pope's "new" theory can be described as departing from Heusler in points two and five, and as introducing the principal tenet of an "initial" rest. A closer examination, however, reveals that Pope is simply resolving the problems of the two-beat theory by returning to the four-beat theory with a free use of rests and rest-beats.

However, the work of Pope should not be underestimated. It is he who brought all the implications of the original four-beat theory, and also of the half-century effort to coordinate Sievers' Five Types with equal time, to a consistent and exhaustive application in *Beowulf*. His choice of two measures rather than four in a half-line, with the result that in many cases of the B and C types of verses the two major stresses both fall in the second measure, is actually a very sensitive response to the rhythmic freedom and sophistication in OE poetry. Pope takes types A, D, and E as supplying the unifying principle of rhythm in the two quadruple measures, as in the following:[19]

9: (A)   wēox under wolcnum weorðmyndum þāh,   (E)

| ♪ ♩ ♩ | ♪ ♩ ⁊ | ♪ ♩ ♩ | ♪ 𝄽 |

10: (A3)   oð þæt him æghwylc ymbsittendra   (D)

| ♪ ♩ ♩ | ♪ ♪ | ♪ | ♪ ♩ ♩ |

Pope treats the B and C verses according to the number of syllables preceding the first stress, as shown in the examples below. In these verses he judges that the first primary stress need not begin the first measure (not even in the b-verses) and demonstrates how in every case where there are three, four, or five unstressed syllables preceding it, the first primary stress actually begins the second measure rather than the first. The preliminary syllables then usually fill the first measure, which as a consequence is more lightly accented than the second, which now contains all the important syllables. The following half-lines illustrate this principle:

1484a: Mǽg þonne òn þǽm gőlde ongìtan   (p. 47)

1809b: sǽgde hìm þæs lĕanes þànc   (p. 56)

1363a: ófer þǽm hőngĭað   (p. 55)

If the three or four syllables do not fill the measure, as is the general rule when there are only two preliminary syllables, the first measure begins with a rest:

56b: (´)òþ þæt hìm ĕft onwŏc   (p. 54)

2260b: (´)Ne mæ̀g bȳrnan hrìng   (p. 54)

When only one syllable precedes the first stress, it may be either the upbeat in the first measure preceded by a rest; or, depending on its relation to the preceding verse, it may be an anacrusis belonging to the time of the preceding measure. One example of each follows:

4a: (´)Òft Scȳld Scĕfing   (p. 57)

220(b): wŭndènstĕfnà | gewădèn hæ̀fdè   (p. 58)

Pope finds this latter explanation to hold true also in some instances with two preliminary syllables.

Pope's work, of course, treats of many details in other types of verses, especially the A3 type, which we have neither the space nor the need to include here. Only one other element is crucial to his theory, and it follows from the use of the initial rest. This is the assumption of the use of a harp in the composition and recitation of *Beowulf*. Pope considers the harp indispensable to his theory because it supplies the first beat of the measure in cases where an initial rest is used in the first measure of the poem and of individual fits. In these cases, he says, the listener could not have supplied the beat from the rhythm of the preceding measure, and it must have been supplied by an outside means, the harp.

If one assumes that a consistent rhythm in poetry demands that it be measurable into a consistent number of equal measures, then John Collins Pope has certainly given the finest and most complete demonstration of the rhythm of *Beowulf*. But the validity of such an assumption is questionable in poetic practice; abstract theory may be another question. Certainly the basic abstract pattern of four members in each half-line of OE poetry may be heard or felt as isochronous, just as the abstract pattern of five iambs in a line of eighteenth-century poetry may be so felt. Either the stresses occur at equal intervals of time or the length of time within like units is felt to be equal, measure to measure, verse to verse. Because a pattern once established takes on something of an archetypal life of its own, there is always a tendency of the sound in poetry toward isochroneity of the pattern; however, the concrete, substantial expression in poetic language will in practice always pull away from the regularity of an abstract pattern. Hence, any system of rhythmic (as opposed to metric) analysis that calls attention to isochronous measurement, as musical notation does, is finally either misleading or presumptuous or both.

Pope's system is both in that he, first of all, bases his theory on the fallacy that rhythm cannot exist outside of strict temporal relation—that rhythm cannot be felt in any two sequences unless they are made equal in time (p. 8). He allows this fallacy to remain in his 1966 edition; however, in the preface to the latter he concedes that "the mathematically exact notation must, of course, be taken as a norm to which actual readings will approach with varying degrees of fidelity" (p. x). Nevertheless, he adds immediately: "Isochrony and initial rests are so vital, in my opinion, for an adequate sense of order in opposition to the extraordinary variety of syllabic patterns in the verses that I cannot take seriously certain counter-proposals, made since 1942, which reject one or both of these features."[20]

Pope's system is further presumptuous in that it assumes the ordinary reader to be capable of an artistic interpretation of modern musical notation. Mensural notation, which began to be adopted in about the twelfth century with the advent of polyphony, was ostensibly based on the rules of classical prosody which regulated durational values, the 2:1 ratios of longs and shorts in the Greek language, into feet of equal time proportions. But among the Germanic people, such a musical system could have come into use only at that turning point when music became a truly separate science from poetry. Durational rhythm was unknown in OE poetry, as witness Bede's attempt to describe the *carmina vulgarium poetarum,* in terms of his own Latin learning, as "compositio non metrica ratione sed numero syllabarum ad judicium aurium examinata."[21] Since this was his own native poetry, he could call it "ad judicium aurium," but the Romans, for example Julian, certainly found it foreign and unpleasant to their ears, and they found it dissonant precisely because it used a different rhythmic principle than that of proportional durations.

Robert Creed in a 1966 PMLA article[22] diluted the isochronous imperative of Pope's system by demonstrating in linguistic symbols rather than in musical notation the six significantly different patterns of stress in Pope's measures. Thus the reader can ignore any implication of isochronous timing and read normally (that is, in irregular rhythm) from his scansion, such as in the following:

B.17:

```
   /    x      /   x       /⌒          x       /    (x)
| wuldres  | Wealdend, | weorold-áre for-  | géaf :

   /    x      /   x      /  (x)      / x      \
| Béow wæs | bróeme  | --bláed   | wíde sprang -- ,
```

However, such a view makes Creed's bar lines nonfunctional, hence annoying; on the other hand, Creed goes to great pains to demonstrate the equation between his measures and those of Pope which are set in musical notation. His "rhythmemes" (pp. 27–31) are good illustrations of the OE poet's freedom to fill one "syllable" position with one, two, or three syllables, or rests; but his assumptions that these would be read as musical doublets or triplets, rather than as binary or ternary groups (little measures on their own), keeps at least his theory fixed in Pope's school of isochronous measures. Nevertheless, I feel that the less musically literate readers of OE will probably use Creed's work as another system of stress-pattern scansion.

THE SCHOOL OF SIEVERS: STRESS-PATTERN SCANNERS

Eduard Sievers originated with his Five Types what became the opposing school of OE prosodists to that of the musical timers. Sievers' system patterns the position of the two strong stresses in relation to the other lesser-stressed and unstressed syllables in a four-member half-line of OE poetry. The Five Types are probably the most widely known and accepted of all OE prosodic descriptions: they have also been incorporated into all the successful systems of timing, as we saw above in the examples of Pope and others. Sievers himself was deeply concerned about timing the rhythm of OE poetry and earlier worked with the other late-nineteenth-century timers; however, in 1893, in the work which came to be regarded as the standard presentation of the Five Types,[23] he took an opposing position, stating that "the attempts of Möller, Heusler, and others to force a definite kind of rhythm and a smooth, even series of bars upon the whole of the AV [alliterative verse] are simply not tenable" (p. 270).

Probably because of the regular rhythm of Western music during the nineteenth and the early twentieth centuries, Sievers concluded that alliterative verse "is subject to the rules of the *spoken* verse (irrational rhythm), which is essentially different from sung verse in that it does not have an invariable rhythm" (p. 270). The principle of free rhythmic alternation on which he believed the verse to be founded he expressed in his system of Five Types. In the typical verses of four members the alternative patterns of equal feet are A⸌x|⸌x, a double falling type; B x⸌|x⸌, a double rising type; and C x⸌|⸌x, a rising-falling type; and alternative patterns of unequal feet: D ⸌|⸌⸌x or ⸌|⸌x⸌ of 1 + 3; and E ⸌⸌x|⸌ or ⸌x⸌|⸌ of 3 + 1. Sievers categorized some twelve subtypes of these according to the position of the secondary stress, as well as one or more extended forms under each type to account for additional members in the verses.

Although Sievers himself probably thought of his system as representing the temporal element in speech—a variable, "irrational" rhythm—the Five Types became for those who adopted them a system for describing simple language patterns of stressed to unstressed syllables with no reference to timing the rhythm they represent. The timers, of course, began almost immediately to incorporate the Five Types into their isochronous measurement. But the Five Types, probably because they were described in terms of feet, also made it possible for scores of OE teachers and scholars in some fifty years after 1893 to limit their understanding of OE rhythm and meter to a somewhat "spatialized" description of language material in a half-line of poetry.

Sievers himself did not stop with this system. His own concern for the temporal element caused him first to theorize on speech melody[24] and finally to change radically and to adopt the principle of regularly recurring measures that "keep time."[25] In order to regularize his timing, however, Sievers often had to ignore the significance of alliteration and normal prose accentuation and to rely on his feeling for speech melody, or what he called *Schallanalyse*. *Schallanalyse* is far too subjective a testing device to have gained popularity among ordinary scholars and teachers of OE. His Five Types, on the other hand, provided a readily accessible and logical system for classifying half-lines since it dealt with the most obvious elements—the stressed and unstressed syllables—and spelt out five simple patterns in which they occur in OE half-lines. Certainly thousands of students and scholars of OE have learned those Five Types without ever questioning their limitations.

A number of theorists in the twentieth century have tried their hands at variations of Sievers' system of recording the language patterns. In 1914, P. Fijn Van Draat tried to show that the Latin "cursus" or prose cadences (the planus: 'xx'x or 'xxx'x; the tardus: 'xx'xx or 'xxx'xx; and the velox: 'xx'x'x) were fundamental to the construction of OE verse. He objected to the importance that Sievers attached to quantity and to secondary stress, and he suggested that there is really a pause-syllable between the two clashing stresses of types C and D.[26] W. W. Greg in 1925 was less success-ful, and certainly less clear, than Van Draat. His endeavor was to distin-guish between different types of theses or *Senkung:* a simple *Senkung,* a simple weighted *Senkung* (with one secondary accent), and a complex weighted *Senkung* (with two secondary accents).[27]

The "centroid" theory advanced by E. W. Scripture in 1928 moved in the direction of laboratory or acoustic metrics. It held that the alliterating groups were centers of gravity for the recurrent swells of energy, the rhythm depending on the number and position of weak syllables in relation to the *Zentroide,* or *Schwerpunkte.*[28] And in 1931 S. O. Andrew tried to prove Sievers wrong, but actually worked in a direct line from him, as a type scanner, by replacing the D and E types with variations of A1 and B1, and reclassifying most of type C as type A2. Andrew said, "Sievers' E type . . . is simply B, (. / | . /), with the first foot weighted. . . . Similarly, Sievers' D type is simply A (/ . | / .), with the first foot weighted."[29]

All of these theories, it seems to me, complicated that of Sievers, although each contained elements of truth that were perhaps most suc-cessfully synthesized by Bliss. Kemp Malone,[30] on the other hand, worked in the direction of simplifying Sievers and of bringing out more graph-ically the simple rhythm of the lines. He did this by classifying OE verses only in terms of the sequences of rhythmical high points they exhibit. The rhythm, he said, grew naturally out of prose rhythm, "by a process of heightening and lowering." And he recognized three kinds of lifts: the major lift, which carries the alliteration, the minor lift, which is stressed but does not alliterate, and the tertiary lift, in which the heightening takes place at a lower level. Malone offered a list of lift patterns in which he distinguished between half-lines with four lifts (the most common) and those with five and even six lifts. Swollen lines such as the latter he attributed to the natural outgrowth of the native metrical tradition, rather than to the invention of clerical writers.

If Kemp Malone saw OE rhythm as a stylization of the natural prose rhythm, Majorie Daunt saw only the prose patterns.[31] She noted in a 1947 work that "what neither Sievers nor any other writers, . . . have ever pointed out, is that the 'five types' are *language patterns,* not *metrical patterns,*" and she then demonstrated how the normal word order of spoken language produces them: "Dissyllabic words such as most nouns, adjectives, and finite verbs were in Old English, naturally combined into A groups, while prepositional phrases, beginning as they do with an un-stressed word followed by a stressed and inflected form, would naturally shape C, important monosyllables would be the foundation of B and three-syllable words the basis of D and E." Daunt's approach would seem to fall between that of Sievers and that of the linguists; she concentrated on speech and language patterns, seemingly without regard for any simple, unifying principle of meter or rhythm that may govern these patterns, yet without using the tools of the linguists, understandably for 1947. That A. J. Bliss in 1958 did not use the linguists' tools while following the same approach is less easily understandable; nevertheless, it is probably he who brought the system of Sievers' Five Types to its most elaborate culmination.[32]

Bliss distinguished between normal, light, and heavy verses. Those containing two elements with linguistic stress he considered normal and used for them the usual capital-letter designations (A, B, C, D, E). Light verses, of which he found 1358, are those which contain "only one stressed element"; if the additional elements in the verse were verbs and/or clitics, he designated these verses with a lowercase letter (a, d, e); if the entire verse contained only a single word—always a compound—he used an italicized capital for designation (*A, D, E*). Heavy verses are those which contain three stressed elements (A*, B*, D*, E*).

An example of each of the categories may be seen in the differentiations of a type A:

1A1a: $\acute{\_}$ | x$\acute{\_}$x	81a: sinc æt symle
a1c: xxx$\acute{\_}$x	9a: oð þæt him æghwylc
1*A*1: $\acute{\_}$:x$\acute{\_}$x	44a: þēodgestrēonum
1A*1a: $\acute{\_}$x | x$\acute{\_}$x	61a: Heorogār ond Hrōðgār

The numbers preceding the letter symbols in the above examples (such as 1A or 3B) designate the position of the caesural pause within the half-line. Bliss called this positioning of the caesura the "most important factor overlooked by Sievers," although in fact his placement agrees with Sievers' in all the verses of type C and of type D, and in more than half of those of types A and E. In those which disagree, the change is made for a syntactical (or morphemic) reason.

Another number is used in Bliss's classification system following the type letter (as 1D3), this one to indicate in some cases the number and length of secondary stresses in the verse, as in the following, which is a normal verse:

    31a: lēof landfruma   1D3: ´ | ´⌣x

and in others the number of unstressed syllables in a drop:

    501b: wæs him Bēowulfes sīð   3B2: xx´xx | ´

With the three-symbol system, Bliss classified fifty different types of verses in *Beowulf*. But by refining the system further to include two additional letters and figures (e.g., 1A1a[i]), he tabulated 130 patterns for 6322 normal verses. The latter symbols have to do with the number of unstressed syllables in expected positions and with short syllables.

The details of Bliss's system, then, are linguistic—the variations in patterns created by different degrees of stress, by the quantitative properties of syllables, and by syntactical phrasing. In view of this fact, W. P. Lehmann in his review of Bliss's book found it regrettable that Bliss's approach to language is one such as "we scarcely expect to encounter today," when the science of linguistics can provide so many helps to such a study.[33] Nevertheless, he accepted Bliss's metrical conclusions.

A dissertation by Elinor D. Clemons in 1961[34] was the first work to test Bliss's system with a scientific linguistic method. Clemons found Bliss's system of scansion "unrealistic in regard to certain aspects of analysis, such as the division of lines into metrical feet and the scansion of certain verbal usages," and proposed a number of rereadings of verses. Rereadings of an entire category of light lines was proposed in an article published in 1967 by Clemons in collaboration with Rudolph Willard.[35]

A major part of the contribution made by Thomas Cable has been in his rereadings of Bliss's lines and a restoration of the types to something of the simplicity of Sievers' originals, but supported by linguistic theory and hypothesis. His first article was focused on the light lines, and restored another category to reading as normal lines.[36] In his 1974 volume, *The Meter and Melody of Beowulf*, on the other hand, he moves back from the catalogs of Bliss, Sievers, and Pope "to inquire about missing patterns. . . . to reveal the principle of exclusion" (*MM* 3), in order to restate the pattern of "metrical order [that] does exist" (*MM* 17).

Cable's conclusions include three concerning stress. Chapter 2 discounts all of Bliss's light verses by arguing that metrical stress is something different from linguistic stress; hence, secondary linguistic stress and, indeed, any syllable that "has greater linguistic prominence than at least one adjacent syllable" (*MM* 27) can fill the position of the second metrical stress in a verse. His first conclusion is that "each verse of Old English poetry contains at least two metrical stresses" (*MM* 30).

His second conclusion is that type E "must contain intermediate stress," and that it is not only "possible to scan most of the words in Bliss's E patterns with intermediate stress," but that "certain unhappy consequences follow if they are not scanned that way" (*MM* 62–63). His third conclusion regarding stress is more closely related to his proposal for a melodic patterning than to a rereading of Bliss's categories. This is the conclusion of Chapter 5 that in Sievers' types C and D "the first of two consecutive stresses must always be the heavier" (*MM* 73).

The constraints Cable finds operating against the use in poetry of many of the normal language patterns found in OE prose—constraints which limit anacrusis, lift the first of two stresses, and demand certain requirements "concerning vowel quantity, resolution, alliteration, and the like" (*MM* 82)—demonstrate the principle of "exclusion" in OE meter. This principle is that every verse, while it has always two metrical stresses, may never have more than four *Glieder,* that is, members or positions. Cable's emphasis on this principle of only four-member verses takes him back to Sievers' original dual emphasis, but it also links his theory to the four-beat theory of the timers, especially as demonstrated by Kaluza and by Pope, who insists on four members although he writes them in two measures.[37]

Continuing his identification with Sievers, Cable offers as a hypothesis that the patterns found in the Five Types are the only ones possible in verses of four members or metrical units. Instead of then allowing the patterns found in feet (always containing two or three members: ´x; x´; ´; ´ ´x; ´x´) to occur in arbitrary combinations, Cable says that rather than feet "a verse has four metrical positions that may occur in any combination, with the condition that the second of two clashing stresses cannot be heavier" (*MM* 89). And this statement, he says, explains why Old English poetry has "exactly five types, rather than four, or six, or three."[38] His symbols for illustrating these patterns are as follows: A: 1＼2／3＼4; B: 1／2＼3／4; C: 1／2＼3＼4; D1: 1＼2＼3＼4; D2 & E: 1＼2＼3／4. I find these confusing (perhaps also misleading) only because no diagonal line follows the 4, thus presuming that 4 is always in the condition of the previous diagonal ending, which is not required in the other positions.

HALLE-KEYSER AND THE OTHER LINGUISTS

Thomas Cable has been one of several critics of metrical theories proposed by linguists,[39] but may have been the most damning when he said, "It is not too much to say that generative prosody has been properly discredited, nor too soon to predict that it will go the way of structural prosody, taking with it the arrows, brackets, symbols, and perhaps the distinct expository style. As in the case of the structural flurry, the final result of the generative activity will probably be a net loss to the progress of English studies" (p. 228).

However, his sweeping statement may apply only to some of the closed systems of analysis that have been proposed. Insights provoked by the linguists, perhaps only from a spirit of antagonism, may have caused metrical theory to move more quickly than it would otherwise have done, considering its centuries within the limitations of classical terminology. But more than this, it is finally only the background work of the linguists on the suprasegmentals—the prosodic features—of language that has provided Cable himself (and also me) with information essential to metrical analysis. Cable has used this information more specifically than even he admits (and he admits a great deal in pages 95–99 of *MM*) in the melodic patterns he posits for Sievers' Five Types.[40] For overriding his careful distinctions between Trager-Smith structural "phonemic stress" and Chomsky-Halle "generative stress" is his clear choice of the distinct pitch levels—his decision that "the main correlate of metrical ictus was relative pitch, and not simply the pitch of ordinary discourse, but a heightened and stylized pattern" (*MM* 95). And he proposes the following melodic patterns to coincide with the five descriptive patterns given above:

A 1↘2↗3↘4

B 1↗2↘3↗4

C 1↗2↘3↘4

D 1↘2↘3↘4

E 1↘2↘3↗4

I see in these melodic patterns at least an analogy to, if not a clear reading of, the pitch levels of the structural linguists.

My appraisal of these melodic patterns should not be read as pejorative. I find them as a whole acceptable, and am especially pleased to have had Cable's careful work on stress to support the patterns in the preceding chapters. However, if they are patterns employed by scops in their performance of the *Beowulf,* they were the performances of only the less talented and imaginative ones. An audience with sensitive ears would have been bored by the frequent interjection of the descending minor third of the A-patterns (the very tones of London's air raid signals, which have now been incorporated into our cities' siren systems), or they would have become irritated by the Bs (which after several repetitions would be like nothing so much as the horn of the Old Fords of the 1930's: ka-zook, ka-zook). I suggest that the more talented scops understood that the prosodic features which go into the linguistic prominence characterizing the stress positions of OE meter could be signaled in a melody by a lower pitch as well as by a higher one. The scops would have known this; we know that their contemporaries who chanted psalms and lessons knew it.[41]

I offered a sample melodic pattern for the reading of *Beowulf* in my 1964 dissertation (p. 132).

It patterned the phrases of the verses in relation to semantic meaning rather than purely in relation to metrical types, following the principles of patterning in liturgical lessons and psalms which a cantor and choir are expected to apply quickly and easily to new material. But I presented that suggestion as a melodic rendering directly related to, or following, the pitch readings done by Mary Lu Joynes, whose 1958 dissertation, "Structural Analysis of Old English Metrics,"[42] probably stands as the most complete application of structural linguistics to OE meter.

Joynes's descriptive scheme recognizes three suprasegmental phonemes as producing the language patterns in the line: stress, juncture, and pitch. She said in regard to the fourth, duration, that "there could be no system of counting of vowel and consonant morae as in Classical Latin or Greek hexameters" (p. 14). Using the three, she described the normal metrical line, "as it may be reconstructed from syntax," as consisting of "four syntactic phrases, each of which has a pitch-juncture morpheme and each of which contains a primary stress" (p. 65). The linguistic formula she used to demonstrate this consists simply of the ' for the lift or *Hebung;* the / | /

juncture (since it is more descriptive than "rest beat," which involves allophonic lengthening of the last preceding major stress rather than silence, which the musical term implies) to indicate the syntactic phrases within thought groups, and the / # / for the end of the sentence; and the three pitch levels (1, 2, and 3). A few lines from the scansion she provided will illustrate this:[43]

```
        2           32      2  22      3      2       22
194: þæt fram hám | gefrǽgn | Hígeláces | þégn |

      32     2    3   2        3    2     2  1
     gód | mid Géatum, | Gréndles | dǽda; #

      2        32     2  2      3    2        2  2
     sē wæs món | cýnnes | mǽgenes | stréngest

     2    32      222    3  2      22
     on þǽm | dǽge | þýsses | lífes, |

     3   2    2   3   1
     ǽþele | ond éacen. #
```

Only primary stress is indicated and this always occurs four times in the full line. Juncture also occurs consistently four times in the full line. Pitch varies from the normal speech tone of /2/ only on the alliterating syllable, where it becomes a /3/, and in conjunction with / # /, when it becomes a /1/.

The linguistic theory of OE prosody presented by Mary Lu Joynes in 1958 has, by her own judgment, "no feature which would contradict earlier metrical analyses such as those of Sievers or Heusler," but is rather "a translation into modern linguistic terms of phenomena which metrists have observed and classified long ago" (p. 67).

In spite of the fact that her system of scanning is descriptive only of language phenomena in structural terms, Joynes does recognize the fact that some unifying principle is present to govern the basic rhythm of the line. By a very skillful and illuminating analysis of the interlinear markings found in the *Beowulf* manuscript, and an interpretation of them in relation to Gregorian Chant, she speculates that "regularization of juncture morphemes" could be the "basic principle of Old English metrics" (p. 80), and she suggests in her concluding chapter that "perhaps further study of music in relation to poetry and the suprasegmental structure of the language involved will reveal that contrary to earlier assumptions, poetry does not derive its form from music, but music derives its form from poetry" (pp. 93–94).

What was most agreeable and useful to me in the information about suprasegmental phonemes provided by the structural linguists, and as utilized by Mary Lu Joynes, was the very formalization and specification which eventually proved its downfall at the hands of succeeding linguists of the transformational and generative models. For art formalizes: music formalizes both the pitches into the vertical patterns of melody and the stresses and durations into the horizontal patterns of metered rhythm; poetry in English usually formalizes only the dominant feature of rhythm into a specific pattern, but the other features are present in the language and may be formalized in any analysis of a performance, or in any theory of the practice in a certain period. Such a practice was that of the OE scop; hence, the attraction to a melodic formalization of the pitches found in speech.

In view of this, I suggest that Cable's melodic patterns fit historically in the school of the linguists, but of the structural linguists, as does much of my previously published work. However, Cable's work as a whole goes beyond this school, and my major emphasis is elsewhere too.

The Halle-Keyser school of OE prosody seems to me to have reached its peak, or culminative definition, in the 1971 volume, *English Stress*.[44] However, we are concerned here with only those pages devoted to "Old English Alliterative Verse" (pp. 147–64) where the rules first set out by Keyser in a 1969 *College English* article were substantially changed and refined. The Abstract Metrical Pattern Rules as refined are stated as follows (p. 153):

> (i) A verse line is composed of a first and second half-line
> (ii) The first half-line is composed of (X)* X
> (iii) The second half-line is composed of X (X)*

The X in the formula may be either an alliterating stress (in which case it is written as S, or a nonalliterating stress (when it is written as W). The asterisk used with the parenthesis indicates that this position may be omitted, and that when it is omitted "the line is more rather than less complex" (p. 149). Since no more than what is represented is necessary, a half-line may be as short as two syllables, and no shorter, and a half-line may have only one stressed syllable. However, it may also be longer, and the Halle-Keyser catalogue includes the following attested patterns (p. 154): in the first half-line: SS, S, SW, WS, SSW, WSS, SWS; in the second half-line: SW, S, SWW, WSW, WS. Combinations of the two half-lines, then, produce thirty-five possible patterns, of which six are unattested.

The Halle-Keyser scansion of stressed syllables is based on assumptions, worked out by Ann Reed, that supposed primary stress for all adjectives, nouns, and verbs (excepting *eom, beon,* and *wesan* in certain conditions);

for most nonclitic adverbs, and for occasional personal pronouns under conditions of emphatic stress. I suggest that these assumptions are entirely linguistical; hence, while they may be useful in ascertaining metrical stresses, those stresses nevertheless will qualify as the two metrical stresses of the OE pattern under constraints that are metrical rather than linguistical. And such constraints may lift a second syllable in a verse to a position of prominence for which it cannot qualify according to the given linguistic assumptions.

Only linguistic evidence is used also to support the Halle-Keyser insistence that the half-line is not an entity: "Bliss's assertion that the half-line is a phonetic entity defined by a pause is false, for there are lines . . . where no pause marks the division into half-lines" (p. 153). The Halle-Keyser School does recognize that "the half-line is a metrical construct, not a syntactic or phonetic entity" (p. 152); but they ignore the validity of the metrical element in the composition of the half-line. Hence, their readings are of full lines, as the following examples show (p. 161):

(a) SSSW   mónegum mǽgþum méodosetla oftéah   (B.5)
             S   S   S   W

(c) SSSWW Béowulf wæs bréme--blǽd wíde spráng   (B.18)
           S   S   S   W   W

(g) SS   þone sélestan sǽcyninga   (B.2382)
              S   S

(s) WSWSW Da cóm ín gân éaldor ðégna   (B.1644)
             W   S   W   S   W

(z) WSSSW   (B.1167)

þæt hē hǽfde mód mícel, þēah þe hē his mágum nǽre
    W   S   S   S   W

The Halle-Keyser theory accommodates many lines emended by editors as unmetrical, and others that stand in the edited texts but which metrists have considered deviant, such as the following (from p. 160):

(a) líssa gelóng; ic lȳt háfo   (B.2150)
    S   S   S   W

(e) hréas blác; hónd gemúnde   (B.2488)
    S   W   S   W

On the other hand, they read as metrically deviant eight lines which do not conform to their "condition" that "if a line contains a line-internal clause or sentence boundary, the boundary must coincide with that of the half-line" (p. 154), which is an interesting refinement of their attitude toward half-line composition. Some of these eight are recognizably different (from p. 157):

(c) Geþénc nu, se mǽra mága Héalfdenes   (B.1474)
     W   S   S   W

(g) éðbegēte þām ðe ǽr his élne forléas   (B.2861)
     S   S   S   W

but others have less obvious differences from the normal half-lines:

(b) Flṓd blṓde wéol—fólc tō sǽgon—   (B.1422)
     S   W   W   S   W

THREE ATTEMPTS AT DETERMINING IRREGULAR RHYTHM

Paull Franklin Baum, Josef Taglicht, and R. B. Le Page seem to have made a more determined effort to come to grips with the problem of demonstrating a free rhythmic structure in *Beowulf* than any of the other scholars who have continued to maintain that its measures are irregular. However, their works differ: Baum never actually provided a system of scansion, as Taglicht and Le Page attempted to do, but on the other hand he brought a broader background of scholarship to bear on the subject and made a far more extensive analysis of the elements involved in the rhythmic structure.[45]

Baum took the half-line, rather than the foot, to be the metrical unit of OE poetry, and he proposed that the two principal stresses with their varying number of accompanying unstressed syllables reduce to one "elastic extensible pattern." This pattern (Sievers' A) is trochaic and admits of four variations which cover Sievers' types C, B, E, and D, in that order.[46] His defense of the trochaic (falling) movement is analogous to the definition of the musical bar line: "all rhythmic groups begin theoretically with the stressed element" (p. 77). He stated that this falling movement is usually produced by a strong stress type of versification, especially when a large proportion of the verses end in an unaccented syllable. The variations are the poet's escape from "the monotony which would result from a regular alternation of stressed and unstressed syllables in a series of heavily accented short verses, with stresses continually emphasized by alliteration."

Baum added that "wider and wider divergences" would give variety and also amuse the scop's "artistic sense—as the ear is teased by dissonances in music and then reassured by a return to the common harmonies." He contended that students of Anglo-Saxon verse have not been willing to recognize (as they have been willing to do with Milton) "that the great variety is only the result of adapting a pattern to the forms of the language in which the poem is composed" (pp. 74, 77, and 82). Baum therefore recognized that two kinds of patterns are in operation, sometimes coinciding and sometimes contending with each other.

A number of further points proposed by Baum, some of which Pope doubtless suggested to him, others of which we have already seen echoed in Bliss and Joynes, deserve mention here. He admitted weak verses containing only one stress, as well as heavy verses with three (which should simply be "read as definitely three-beat"). In regard to alliteration, he showed that double alliteration does occur in b-verses, that it is sometimes used for enjambment, that alliteration (and metrical stress without it) frequently falls on "small" words and syllables which are not necessarily stressed, that even when it is nonfunctional it attracts attention, and finally and most dramatically, that alliteration on occasion may not be on the first stress of the b-verse.

In this final point he distinguished between the first "strong accent and the first metrical stress" and advanced a logical step beyond Pope, whom he quoted as saying, "If the first measure of the second half-line is weakly accented, the alliterating syllable can begin the second measure without ceasing to be the first of the two strongest syllables in the line." [47] Baum admitted with Joynes as well as with Pope that "syllabic length in metrical reading does not necessarily inhere in the word itself, but equally in the delivery." And in his final section he argued that the hypermetric lines are no different from many other lines and would not be noticed if, instead of being grouped together, they simply appeared "in the second half of non-hypermetrical lines" (pp. 91, 158, and 160).

In his discussion of possible musical analogies to a free rhythmic interpretation of *Beowulf,* Baum buries in a footnote a comment that would seem to deserve more attention:

Bede defined the *carmina vulgarium poetarum* as "compositio non metrica ratione sed numero syllabarum ad judicium aurium examinata" ("De arte metrica," *Miscellaneous Works,* ed. Giles, VI, 77 ff. . . .) This reminds one of the plainsong, in which, according to some, the syllables were sung with equal time-values. The *judicium aurium* is also subject to interpretation, Julian having found the songs of the Germans unpleasant to his ears, though satisfying to the natives. *Rhythmus* as a name for vernacular verse sometimes . . . describes a syllable-counting meter and sometimes a *modulatio sine ratione,* i.e., nonquantitative. Syllable-counting the meter of the *Beowulf* certainly is not (p. 75).

But Baum does not explore the plainsong, or Gregorian Chant, of which he is reminded. In his text he implies that he cannot do so because there is not a universally accepted explanation of the rhythmic values, "some holding that the syllables had equal time-values; others that the rhythm was measured by melodic elevation and divided into freely mingled binary and ternary groups; still others that the notes represent actual duration and are arranged in groups of two to eight beats" (p. 75), and he is not in a position to judge for himself in the matter.

One dissertation at least, that by Eva Katherine Touster,[48] sprang from Baum's study. Touster found it impossible, however, to evolve a clear and accurate system for demonstrating her principles. Instead, her work on the movement in normal and heavy verses (which she classified as level, level-descending, descending-ascending, and descending-ascending-descending, changing the meaning of some of Sievers' letters) became a study in diction rather than one in rhythm or meter as such, taking one closer to the matter of Adeline C. Bartlett's *The Larger Rhetorical Patterns in Anglo-Saxon Poetry*.[49] Furthermore, in her more valuable first chapter on the previous theories, her divisions into *Gesungen-vers* and *Spreche-vers* is based on the assumption that singing can be done only in isochronous measures in which a melody dominates the words.

It was precisely a recognition of the existence of "all sorts of musical rhythms very different from the isochrony which has dominated European music for so long a time" that enabled Josef Taglicht to advance somewhat further toward a system of scanning free rhythm. By demonstrating irregular measures in English folksongs, in addition to noting the better known examples in Gregorian Chant and in music of Eastern Europe, Africa, and other parts of the world, Taglicht brought his argument in more direct line with the Germanic tradition. By utilizing the comparative values found in such music in conjunction with the linguistic and metrical evidence in the poetry itself, he concluded that the meter of *Beowulf* has a chronometric framework, within which the "verse rhythm is based essentially on the rhythm of speech" (p. 349). Taglicht added that the second clause invalidates "any solution which attributes the same duration to phonemically long and short sounds under identical conditions of stress and phrasing." As a result, Taglicht's system of scansion fixes quantity on syllables but recognizes their distribution into irregular measures. And whereas he assumed an equal amount of time (four beats) to half-lines composed of A, D, and E types, he assigns an indeterminate quantity to half-lines of types B, C, and A3. The symbols he used with their respective values are these: $|$ = 1, $\lceil$ = $1\frac{1}{2}$, $\|$ = 2, $\lceil\lceil$ = $2\frac{1}{2}$, and x stands for a variable number of syllables which do not include a primary or secondary stress. A few lines representing each type illustrate this system (pp. 350–51):

1. ‖ + ‖ (Sievers' A)
   13a: ‖ geóng in ‖ géardum
   720a: ‖ còm þa to ‖ récede
   301a: ge ‖ wìton him þa ‖ féran
2. ⌐ + ⫟ (Sievers' D)
   31a: ⌐ léof ⫟ lándfrùma
   78b: ⌐ scòp him ⌐ Héort | náman
   9b: ⌐ + ⫟ ýmbsìttèndra
3. ⫟ + ⌐ (Sievers' E)
   8b: ⫟ wéorðmỳndum ⌐ þáh
   545a: | fíf ⌐ níhta ⌐ fýrst
4. x + ‖ (Sievers' A3)
   53a: þa wæs on ‖ búrgum
5. x + ⫟ (Sievers' B and C)
   34a: a ⫟ lédon þà
   1b: in ⫟ geárdàgum
   441b: se þe hine ⌐ déað | nímeð

Some four years before Taglicht's system appeared in print, R. B. Le Page had proposed a metrical framework for the Five Types that does not assign quantity to syllables, but rather what he called "weight, a complex perhaps of duration, stress, emotional significance and so on" (p. 99). Le Page utilized Baum's study and made some important additions and modifications. For example, he took the rhythmical unit in *Beowulf* to be the full line, not the half-line, because only in the complete line can there be "that compensation of weight between one 'foot' and another which preserves the spoken rhythm of type D," for example; and only in its context can a satisfactory statement be made "about the combination which has, as its second half, a type B with extended first dip" (p. 101). In agreement with Baum, and in opposition to Pope, Le Page suggested that in any adequate notation "it is necessary to allot to certain half-lines three bars, not two," and further that "the time-signature is liable to vary"— which variation he considered "an essential part of the *Beowulf* poet's technique" (p. 96).

More fundamentally than this, Le Page took issue with the postulate that rhythm implies an obvious beating of time—as Thomson suggested by his "tapping test." [50] By using the results of laboratory studies published previous to Thomson's work, Le Page showed that "carried out by the reciter himself" such tapping "at once distorts the natural rendering of the lines and imposes a falsely-isochronous pattern on the verse" (p. 93). In proposing his own simple rhythmic scansion for a few lines of *Beowulf*, then, Le Page attempted to represent only a "mental ictus." There is no need, he said, "to give an additional stress to a syllable because it coin-

cides with the ictus," thus indicating that there is a regular rhythmic return
of the ictus independent of the two principal stresses in the half-line,
which is a result of the norm established in the mind "by the preponderance of A-type half-lines." The norm consequently is not lost even though
the variations to which it is susceptible are "extremely subtle and complex." Le Page scanned only eight full lines of *Beowulf* in his article, but
used a passage that includes all five types in nice variation. In the three I
am reproducing below, the line above the verses represents the continuous
flow of time, and the arrows indicate the mental ictuses. The acute accents
over syllables are those of the Five Types.

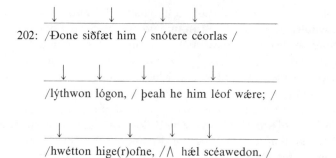

202: /Ðone siðfæt him / snótere céorlas /

/lýthwon lógon, / þeah he him léof wǽre; /

/hwétton hige(r)ofne, /∧ hǽl scéawedon. /   (p. 102)

Le Page's scansion, although I am quite sympathetic to it, reminds me
of Sievers' *Schallanalyse;* it is probably too subjective to be useful to very
many readers. The same is true of the systems of Taglicht and of Baum.
All use individually devised symbols. Pope, on the other hand, may have
been as successful as he was simply because he employed the interna-
tionally used signs of modern musical notation. However, his very use of
this system raises two serious problems.

First of all, the notation system of Western music was standardized in
early modern times for scoring regularly measured music. The notes and
the rests are signs of specific durational values, and they are distributed
into bars of equal time fixed by the time signature. The notation system
itself was designed on the principles of Greek prosody and developed
when music became a separate science from song and poetry,[51] after the
close of the OE period. Historically there is no reason to believe that the
songs and poetry of the Germanic peoples were rendered according to the
timing this notation represents. We have no records of regularly measured
music from Anglo-Saxon times.

On the other hand, we do have records of another kind of music in use
in the Anglo-Saxon kingdoms during the OE centuries. This is the Gregorian Chant, the irregularly timed music to which several of the above

prosodists referred.[52] Peter Clemoes has shown, for example, that both punctuation and chant notation developed from the markings used in early manuscripts to signal a reader or cantor.[53] In addition modern research into the origins and the development of Gregorian Chant provides claims which support a use of chant notation to demonstrate the irregularly timed rhythm of OE poetry.

However, I do not use chant notation, because its application to poetry would raise what is also the second problem raised by Pope's use of modern musical notation: musical notation is for music, not for poetry. It was applied to poetry historically in an attempt to define those qualities in language which linguistics has since distinguished as the prosodic features, and has clarified as to their operation in language. But musical notation can never be wholly successful for scanning poetry, because it defines the pattern of sound (as distinct from words) primarily, and that of words only incidentally. For music is an arrangement of sounds primarily and of words only secondarily and incidentally, whereas poetry is first of all the art of verbal language and then necessarily but secondarily the art of sounds as they inhere in that language.[54] Thus there is little value in proposing the use of another, less widely known, though authentic, musical notation system for scanning the rhythm of OE poetry. And this may have been the reason that the previous scholars who made reference to Gregorian Chant did not attempt to do so.

However, there can be a very real value in investigating the principle of irregularity in the rhythm of Gregorian Chant and in demonstrating the analogy between that principle and the one operating in language. This is what I do in chapter 2 of this book. At the same time in chapter 2, I suggest the use of metrical and linguistic, rather than musical, symbols for scanning the measurement of the irregularly-timed verses of *Beowulf*.

2 THE UNEQUAL MEASURES OF GREGORIAN CHANT

John Collins Pope and other musical scanners of English poetry have generally limited themselves to the musical system of Western culture of the modern centuries. Hence their scansions have assumed time signatures governing measures separated by bar lines which have no other function than to exert a certain tyranny in equalizing the time in the measures. Although many contemporary musicians have freed themselves from the "tyranny of the bar line" and now employ shifting time signatures of irregular numbers ($\frac{9}{8}$ $\frac{3}{4}$ $\frac{17}{8}$) in succeeding measures, most musicians and probably all laymen in music from the sixteenth through the nineteenth centuries assumed that time signatures were only rarely changed in a piece and that they were limited to ratios reducible to either $\frac{2}{4}$ or $\frac{3}{4}$. Along with this assumption arose the fallacy that rhythm demands equal timing.

But long before the sixteenth century there was Western music that had no regular beat. There was, of course, the Gregorian Chant, to which we will devote most of this chapter, which took its original inspiration from the likewise irregular Byzantine and Hebrew chants. The initial efforts in Latin psalmody were brought to the Anglo-Saxon and Germanic world by the cantors who accompanied and followed Augustine of Canterbury; but what became the repertoire of Gregorian Chant developed chiefly in Germanic and Frankish monasteries.[1] There were also during the Middle English centuries the free-wheeling folksongs to which Taglicht and Cable refer in the articles cited in chapter 1 above. From chant and folksongs there evolved the more intricate polyphony and madrigals and the other irregular rhythms of the Renaissance, which Curt Sachs describes as "quite unintelligible" when "seen from the limited viewpoint of the nineteenth century."[2] But Sachs goes on to say that these irregular rhythms are quite natural when interpreted in terms of Eastern music or of Greek dochmiacs and of primitive rhythms, all of which he treats at some length in his study of music history.

In order to learn about measuring the irregular rhythms of OE I have chosen, from among all of these kinds of music, to investigate Gregorian Chant. My choice rests on several reasons. First of all, Gregorian Chant is the music to which most OE scholars have referred as having the rhythmic feel of OE poetry. Secondly, it was sung and composed by the Germanic and Frankish people and used in the Anglo-Saxon monasteries during the centuries which are called the Golden Age of Anglo-Saxon poetry.[3] Finally, there has been a wealth of research in the last century on Gregorian Chant rhythm.

This chapter will draw from this research, first of all to provide a description and illustration of chant rhythm, and secondly to distinguish between the schools of Gregorian Chant rhythm. We will then use the theory of the Solesmes school to investigate rhythm under three headings: the material of rhythm, the analysis process or rational measurement, and the synthesis or composite rhythm. In each we will draw the analogy between the element in chant theory and its counterpart in general linguistic theory.

CHANT RHYTHM

Chant rhythm is entirely different from the rhythm of nineteenth-century music. The word *different* should not, however, be confused with *difficult*. Chant rhythm can be very simply described as mixed binary *and* ternary. To relate this to modern metrical terms, a trochee is in English poetry a binary foot, that is, composed of two pulses of time, or syllables (although it was not binary in Greek, of course); and a dactyl is a ternary foot, that is, composed of three pulses of time, or syllables. Modern music is binary when it is written in signatures such as $\frac{2}{8}$, $\frac{4}{8}$, or $\frac{4}{4}$ time; $\frac{3}{8}$ time on the other hand is ternary.

Chant "time" is a free mixing of the two: little measures of two pulses may be followed by little measures of three. Below is an example of figured chant (the neumatic type) to which I have supplied the count of the binary and ternary measures to illustrate this free mixing.[4] Every count of "1" is known as an ictus—that is, it begins a new little measure—and because there are more notes than syllables the ictus is used in the melodic line rather than in the text. I have also supplied the same piece in modern notation for those who find the chant notation foreign.[5]

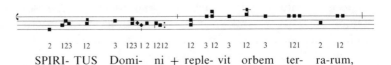

```
   2   123   12      3  123 1 2 1212      12   3 12   3    12   3      121    2   12
   SPIRI- TUS    Domi-  ni + reple- vit    orbem   ter-  ra-rum,
```

The elements which make up the rhythm as illustrated above fall into three categories or levels. First, there is the element of the material comprising movement; in the audible phenomena of the examples, these are the melodic notes and rests together with the words that accompany them. The second element is the analysis—the measures, each beginning with an ictus—which has been imposed by the intellect for the purpose of ordering the material into units which can then be apprehended as equal or unequal. The third element is rhythm proper, the element of synthesis which gathers up the little measures into the larger movement. This in no way has been marked visually above, but will be given later in the chapter. My demonstration of these three elements in the rhythm of Gregorian Chant will follow the theory worked out by monks of the Solesmes Abbey in France.

THE SOLESMES SCHOOL OF CHANT RHYTHM

My choice of the Solesmes school does not ignore the fact that there have also been two other modern schools of Gregorian Chant rhythm—the accentualists and the mensuralists—a fact which stopped Baum from pursuing his conviction that *Beowulf* rhythm is like that of the chant.[6] The confusion of three schools must be transcended in the same way we transcend differing schools of prosody, that is, by recognizing the principle on which each operates. Very simply these are as follows: the accentual-ists[7] use the stress-accent in the text line to determine the ictus in counting their measures; the Solesmes school[8] tends to equalize the syllables by using a melodic accent equally with a stress accent, thus providing the ictus mark in the musical line rather than in the text line (as shown in the first example); and the mensuralists[9] use the rules of Greek prosody to affix durational values to notes and syllables according to the 2 : 1 ratio of long to short.

Obviously, the mensuralists can provide no help to the OE prosodist unless classical durational values are affixed onto English words. The theories of both the accentualist and the Solesmes schools, on the other hand, can provide models for counting irregularly measured rhythms. However, the Solesmes method probably represents more intense and meticulous scholarly research over a longer period.[10] Beginning as they did in the middle of the nineteenth century to recover and restore the thousands of medieval manuscripts of chant melodies, these monks found themselves working with material whose rhythmic nature was at total variance with all that was understood and practiced as rhythmically correct in the musical and prosodical world of their time. As the beauty of this style began to emerge from their conscientious effort at restoration, they were impelled to seek an explanation for its strange, fluid beauty. In presenting the results of their efforts to the Church and to the musical world, they were literally forced to analyze systematically and thoroughly the character and the origin of rhythm in general in order to establish the authenticity of this different kind of rhythm.

The works that contain the Solesmes theory of rhythm are principally by Dom André Mocquereau:[11] *Le Nombre musical grégorien,* in two volumes and three parts, and much of the fourteen volumes of *Paléographie musicale,* volume seven of which treats of rhythm. The important work that preceded Mocquereau's was Dom Joseph Pothier's *Les Melodies grégoriennes.* Some of the more valuable works that have followed Mocquereau's, aiming rather at clarification than at augmentation, are those by Dom Gregory Suñol: *Introduction à la paléographie musicale grégorienne* and *Textbook of Gregorian Chant According to the Solesmes Method;* by Dom Joseph Gajard: *The Solesmes Method: Its Fundamental Principles and Rules of Interpretation* and *The Rhythm of Plainsong According to the Solesmes School;* and the collection of articles by A. Le Guennant, *Préces de rhythmique grégorienne d'après des principes de Solesmes* (1952). Le Guennant's is actually one of the last works to bring together all that had been said before, but with a view to the difficulties that had been encountered in half a century of teaching Gregorian Chant rhythm.

Since my aim in this study is to give OE scholars enough experience in the field of Gregorian Chant rhythm to satisfy the speculation of the last three decades, I will follow almost exactly the method set up by Mocquereau in four steps from analysis to synthesis, progressing from an understanding of the primary or simple beat, to that of simple rhythm, then the compound beat, and finally composite rhythm. I shall deviate only slightly from this method in my demonstration of chant rhythm, using three steps instead of four. In doing so I am following principally Joseph Gelineau, S. J., whose *Voices and Instruments in Christian Worship*[12] appeared in the early 1960's, when the interest in a vernacular music for Catholic worship impelled many musicians to revise the method in order to clarify the principles behind this surpassingly fitting liturgical vehicle. However, this method differs only in that it links the discussion of primary rhythm and of the compound beat under one heading, which Gelineau calls the "rational measure." A separate presentation of primary rhythm is useful only when we deal with the classical feet as separate entities.

My presentation will move as quickly as possible from the chant concept of each of the three elements—primary beat, rational measure, and composite rhythm—to an application to English metrical theory. In doing so, I will transcend the differences between syllabic chant (one note to each syllable, as in the lessons and psalms), neumatic chant (groups of notes on a syllable), and melismatic chant (long melodic phrases on a single syllable, as in the Alleluias). For the principle behind all of them is the same—a free mixing of binary and ternary measures—whether they be groups of syllables (syllabic chant) in which the ictus falls on the linguistic feature dominating words in that language, or groups of musical sound (neumatic and melismatic chant) in which the ictus is governed principally by tonic and durational features.

THE MATERIAL OF RHYTHM: THE SIMPLE BEAT OR PULSE

The Gregorian Chant masters, in text, handbook, and classroom, always began their presentation with the following illustration of the material of rhythm.

The material of temporal rhythm—that is, rhythm occurring in time, such as in music and poetry—will be any of the sounds that *move* time. Time of course is discernible only through the things that take place within it. Sounds are such things. For the sake of illustrating this phenomenon we might represent the continuity of time by a continuous line of indefinite length.

The emission of a single phoneme or syllable can divide this time:

_____ la _____

But if the sound once emitted is indefinitely sustained, the ear could no longer measure its flow. To produce the sense of marking time, the sound must be repeated at intervals neither too far apart for the memory and mind to measure them, nor too close together (as in the roll of a drum) to distinguish them. The repetition of a vowel, with either an unvoiced glottal stop or a consonant, produces this effect, as would the continued striking of a key on a piano or the tick of a clock:

la la la la la la la la la la la la la la la la la la
 | | | | | | | | | | | | | | | | | |

There is no rhythm here; these are simply individual sounds juxtaposed, and time merely moves from one to the next. This individuated sound is usually called either the beat or the pulse. In modern music it is called a note or rest. In Gregorian Chant notation, this note is called the *punctum,* which came to be represented by the square note ▄▄▪▄▄ only after the eleventh or twelfth century when the chant was already in its decline. Before that, the punctum was simply a point (·) such as we are accustomed to seeing in the manuscripts of OE, or sometimes a virgule-like stroke (/) that became a neum. These were placed between the text lines over the words at various heights to indicate pitch, but musical staff lines were not used until the eleventh century.

The usefulness of the chant punctum to us is in its definition. It is the indivisible primary unit of sound whose *relative* duration is governed by the length of the syllable to which it is joined, or its equivalent in melismatic chant.

Very often, only one open note ⎯▱⎯ is found in lessons and psalms (as in operatic recitatives) which indicates that the words are to be given their relative values. At other times, a line of Latin words has square notation above it, as in the psalm verse

Dixit   Dominus   Domino   meo: sede   a   dextris   meis

But this does not indicate that each syllable is of equal length. In theory, each is as long as the syllable to which it is attached. Hence, a Roman using classical pronunciation would give the long Latin syllables twice the length of the short. Historically, few other than Romans spoke Latin this way, and this fact accounts for the development of chant as it occurred north of the Alps. However for modern French choirs, this equalization has been natural because of the nature of their native language; while for English- and German-speaking choirs the result of such an interpretation was a wooden sound.

The notation systems in neumatic, better than syllabic chant, can provide something of an abstract notion of the relative duration of this indivisible primary unit; for chant notation has what are called liquescent notes, ⎯▰▰▰⎯, the smaller notes in neums, which though shorter
12 123 123
than the other notes are nevertheless given the same "relative" count. It is a vocal nuance, like a linguistic enclitic or a syllabic consonant, and defies accurate translation into modern notation, although glissandos are close approximations. In similar attempts at translation, the square note has been rendered as an eighth note (♪) (indeed, some musicians refer to a punctum as a *brevis*), but a liquescent cannot be accurately transcribed as a sixteenth note.

An analogy to the differences signified here may be found in words of a language in which duration is not specified. Hence, in the first neum the two notes might have the durational difference of the two syllables in the OE *hwīle;* that is, the long syllable is longer than the second, but not precisely so much longer as to be given two counts, even though an individual's performance may make it that. I might suggest for the second neum the OE word *cyninga,* or the ModE *library;* and for the third neum the OE *fremedon,* or the ModE *crucifix.*

Slight lengthening is also provided for in neumatic notation. The *quilisma* (the jagged note between two ascending notes) indicates for ordinary choirs that the note preceding it is slightly lengthened, but not as much as two beats: ▬▬▪▪ . Analogous to the neum with a quilisma might be the OE *heofones.* The Solesmes scholars also added a rhythmical mark called the horizontal *episema* to indicate slight lengthening: ▬▪▪▪ ; this is never to be interpreted as lasting two counts. Analogous to the two neums as given might be the OE *Hrunting beran.* Of course, putting words on the neums is misleading, since by definition a neum is a group of notes over one syllable. My analogies are between melodic groups (as such) and syllabic groups (as such).

If the punctum is not divisible in chant, it is however additive. Lengthening to two or three beats is always possible, and is indicated by the use of a dot with the punctum (▪.), the *distropha* (▪▪), *tristropha* (▪▪▪), and all the neums that constantly occur in anything other than the simplest syllabic chant.

Still, it is the concept of the punctum as the indivisible primary unit of sound with relative durational value that is most useful to the English prosodist. English words do not have fixed durational values either; hence the use of any symbol that fixes duration is misleading. Timing them must be conceived in relative terms, as with the punctum in chant psalmody. Using a punctum, however, is not particularly desirable—certainly not the square note of later centuries; and the point used in the early manuscripts would not be readily understood. What is acceptable to prosodists and linguists as standing for a syllable is the "x," and it is usually understood to have the same temporal significance as the punctum does in syllabic chant. The "x" then in my demonstration signifies the syllabic material of movement in sound with relative durational value.

Syllables, however, are not the only material that moves in sound. In the continued marking of time, the individual beats or pulses may be filled by either sound or silence. Mocquereau called pauses "elements of rhythmic composition in the same degree as are the sounds which they replace;"[13] however, Mocquereau was not speaking of rest beats as they are signified in modern notation.

The terminology in chant theory can be misleading, because pauses are marked by what are called bars: the quarter bar (▬▬), the half bar (▬┼▬), and the full bar (▬┼▬) . These have no relation to bars in modern musical notation, nor are they very close in significance to rests. Indeed, their equivalence is not to musical terms, but to language phenomena; they are what in language are called boundaries. The quarter bar is equivalent to a syllable or word boundary; the half bar is closest to a phrasal boundary, although this may be either a semantic (even emphatic) phrase of very short segments or a syntactic phrase; and the full bar is equivalent to the terminal boundary of a clause or sentence.

The amount of time assigned to the bars of Gregorian Chant is very important since this is formalized art. However, only the half bar and the full bar constitute pulses of time; that is, only they are counted into the measures. The quarter bar is for phrasing only and is never given time in the counting, nor does it allow for a breath. Good singers of the chant do not use the half bar for breathing time either, and conductors never allow a breath stop at the half bar. However, the half bar does represent one pulse of time. This pulse may be the second or third count in a measure, or it may constitute the ictus—the downbeat or first count of a new measure whose first note is then an upbeat. That is how the half bar functions in the following phrase taken from the *Christus Factus Est* sung during Holy Week:

pro no - bis   o-be - di-ens

Again, choirs are always warned not to exceed the one beat of time allowed for the half bar. Thus, if someone is forced to grab a breath, he must be ready to come in on "2" of the measure.

The full bar in chant is a sentence boundary; hence it may better be called a pause, or break. Within the chant piece, it is not an indefinite pause, but constitutes one measure of time, that is, two or three pulses. Thus, full bars mark time, as they do also in continuing speech (or more correctly, recitation). If I continue the example from the *Christus Factus Est* from where it left off above, we will have good examples of both the quarter bar and the full bar as they "count" in chant movement:

di-ens us-que ad   mor - tem,   mor-

At the same time, the quarter bar in the example functions as the boundary of a phonological unit, hence as a potential break.

Just as I accepted above the notion of the chant punctum but chose to use the prosodic symbol "x" to represent syllable-sound in the movement of OE poetry, so I take the concept of the chant bars but use modified prosodic symbols to represent in OE poetry what is better described as boundaries and line breaks.[14] I derived these symbols from a combination of the bars of Gregorian Chant; from the boundary symbols of linguistics, although mine are closer to the old juncture symbols of the structural linguists; and from the symbols available on most typewriters. Thus, a | represents one pulse of time (although the available / may be used instead) and I call this a single-bar boundary. Doubled (‖ or //) it represents two pulses of time and I call it a double-bar boundary. It is convenient, particularly in scanning OE poetry, to cross the double bar when a sentence is terminated with a period, since that represents a terminal break that does not expect continuation, and the time involved may be more indefinite. I do use the # in these instances, but recognize the confusion possible in such usage, since the # is used for the smallest boundary units in transformational and generative linguistics.

How these bar symbols appear and are counted in the measurement of an OE verse is illustrated in the following example:

    hu þa æðelingas | ellen fremedon #[15]
    1   2   1 2 1   2   3 1   2   1 2 3 12

The boundaries represented by the symbols | ‖ # (or / // #) are those which constitute the line breaks in the formalization of speech into verse. Thus they become metrical symbols, signaling metrical units used for the purposes of metrical scanning. In OE verses, of course, their linguistic function usually coincides with their metrical function, but when it does not, the symbol maintains its metrical significance and loses the linguistic one.

The distinction is necessary since there is another linguistic boundary that occurs within the verses of OE poetry and constitutes a pulse of time, thus becoming a part of metrical analysis also. This is the situation within a verse when two ictuses immediately follow each other, as in *bát bánlocan*. If I were to choose neums that are analogous to the rhythm of this verse, I would use either a dotted punctum (•.) or a distropha (••), both of which take two counts, for *bán,* and then a *cephalicus* (•ʼ) for *bánlocan*. Giving the extra pulse to *bán* is the natural way to handle this situation of two ictuses occurring together. The extra pulse is not caused by the length of the long vowel but by the necessity of an upbeat before the following ictus could occur. Musicians have no trouble adding this pulse, since they have known for a long time that there cannot be two consecutive downbeats without an upbeat intervening. Hence, they simply lengthen the first downbeat into what becomes a little measure. It is more difficult to find linguistic terminology to describe what occurs in speech. Nevertheless, it is the transition time of the word boundary that is required in order to stress two consecutive syllables; and this time constitutes a full pulse.

To indicate this pulse of time, the symbol must be different from that used for the one-pulse line break if the clarity and importance of the line units are not to be impaired. A half-bar symbol (ı) could be used (like the half bar of chant) but since it is not readily available I have adopted the plus sign (+) which is now on most expanded typewriter keyboards. Again there can be confusion with the boundary that the + symbolizes in generative linguistics. For my purposes it is a metrical symbol for what may be called a line-internal boundary representing a pulse of time, as

        Oft Scyld+Scefing.
        2   1 2   1 2

In addition to the situation of two consecutive ictuses, the + may also be used to represent a line-internal phrasal boundary occurring within the line unit, as in the following:

    272b: # þu w a s t , + g i f   h i t   i s |
              1   2   1   2   1   2   1   2

    1810a: cwæð, + h e   þ o n e   g u ð + w i n e |
               1   2   1   2 3   1   2   1 2 3

THE ELEMENT OF ANALYSIS: THE RATIONAL MEASURE

We have already been using such terms above as *binary* and *ternary* groups and *measures,* as well as *ictus* which begins such groups with a downbeat. Here we want to investigate the concept of such grouping, and we will again first do so in the plodding methodology of the chant masters.

A succession of identical sounds—notes and rests, or syllables and boundaries—may constitute the *material* of rhythm, but they do not constitute rhythm. Timed rhythm is first of all a grouping of sounds by the human mind, which recognizes the recurrence of some feature in some of the sounds as different from others. In the abstract, this feature may be any one of many, such as the linguists' suprasegmental phonemes—stress, duration, and pitch—which are also called the rhythmic or prosodic elements of language.[16]

For example, if we take the undifferentiated series of primary beats given on page 36 above, and stress every second sound as in the following example, we have grouped them in twos—we have set up a relationship of strong to weak in a binary pattern:

        lā lá lā lá lā lá lā lá

On the other hand, if we give equal stress to every pulse but lengthen every second one to twice the length of the first, we have produced a rhythmic group by means of duration, and incidentally have a ternary pattern:

$$\overline{\text{la}}\ \overline{\text{la-a}}\ \overline{\text{la}}\ \overline{\text{la-a}}\ \overline{\text{la}}\ \overline{\text{la-a}}\ \overline{\text{la}}\ \overline{\text{la-a}}$$

We can do the same by means of pitch indication, alternating between /2/ and /3/, for example, in a binary pattern.

The theory of rhythm on this level as worked out by the Solesmes scholars for Gregorian Chant is far more elaborate than we need for use with poetry. Their work was complicated by the fact that they were dealing with a language whose rhythm in classical theory was determined by duration but in practice was often given a stress accent that was probably originally a pitch accent; and the scholars were trying to see the relationship between this language accent and the ictus they found in the melodic neums, which their theory finally interpreted as tonic and durational. However, one of their early conclusions which is helpful to prosodists in the understanding of rhythm was expressed more clearly by one of the scholars who followed him than by Mocquereau himself:

If I can obtain rhythm by means of intensity without the aid of duration, then duration is not essential to rhythm. Similarly, if I can obtain rhythm by means of duration without the aid of intensity, then neither is intensity essential to rhythm. Hence rhythm can exist apart from intensity, apart from duration, and even apart from melody, provided it be determined by some other element. If, therefore, it can exist without any of the elements given, it is evident it is not to be identified with any one of them.[17]

This theory is true of rhythm as such, and explains why the Solesmes theorists always called any feature imparting rhythm the ictus. But as soon as one's native language becomes the rhythmic material, that language's dominant feature becomes recognized as recurring to form the basic rhythmic movement. This dominant feature varies with different languages: rhythm in classical Greek was determined by the suprasegmental phoneme of duration, which means that the length of the long syllables was the recurring feature recognized by the hearer; in Chinese it is determined by tone, or pitch; that is, one hears the rhythm in the recurrence of the higher pitch; in English the dominant rhythmic feature is stress.

As soon as we begin to talk about stress in English we are forced to make distinctions about kinds of stress—the kind that includes only phonemic stress, which is probably intensity; or the kind that exhibits intensity, frequency, and duration—and distinctions about levels: primary, secondary, and such.[18] For the sake of staying as close as possible to the theory of the chant masters, I will make the distinctions follow their sequence.

In language it is lexical (word-level) stress that creates the primary grouping. Primary groups become measures when a number of them are strung together; but when one stands alone there exists what the chant masters call primary rhythm. Any of the two- and three-note neums we used on p. 37 constitutes a primary rhythm in chant. When we turn to speech material, it is the two- or three-syllable word that is the best example of primary rhythm, as found, for example, in the following when each is said in isolation: dáily, yésterday, todáy, tomórrow. Ilse Lehiste provides me with the most accommodating explanation of what occurs in the pronunciation of these words, and one that fits the chant explanation, when she says that "the minimal unit of contrastive stress placement is a sequence of two syllables."[19] However, even this contrast may be a "perceptual reality [only] for those who know the language"; hence, word-level stress is "an abstract quality: a potential for being stressed" (p. 150). When this potential is realized by the words being given emphatic pronunciation in isolation, the stressed syllable gathers up, so to speak, the lesser stressed or unstressed syllables around it[20] to produce the patterns of primary rhythm recognized as the classical feet of poetry. For example, *dáily* is a trochee; *yésterday* a dactyl; *todáy* an iamb; and *tomórrow* an amphibrach. And we can find the same "feet" in OE words: *dágum, frémedon, gebád, gefrúnon.*

Ordinarily we do not use words in isolation; we are more concerned about what happens to word-level stress when we have lengths of more than three syllables. Polysyllabic words offer the first clue. American dictionaries, for example, usually provide a secondary stress mark for every polysyllabic word and for words of three syllables when the primary stress falls on either the first or the last: métaphòr, mètaphóricàl, sécondàry, láboratòry, extráordinàry. These are ictuses. But again, these ictuses are heard as stresses only when the words are spoken in isolation; otherwise, Lehiste says that such stress is only "the capacity of a syllable within a word to receive sentence stress when the word is realized as part of the sentence" (p. 150).

Lehiste uses the term *sentence stress* for the kind of stress that provides the composite rhythm in English speech, and this will be discussed later in this chapter. We are more concerned at this point with the fact that syllables continue to retain their capacity as ictuses even when grouped in larger rhythmic units, and that this capacity when realized in either emphatic or somnorific recitation will reveal such an ictus recurring on every second or third syllable.

Peter Ladefoged suggests that students apply the tapping test[21] in order to recognize how stresses recur at these short intervals. Although I find the principle behind a tapping test erroneous—we can impose isochroneity in the process of tapping—nevertheless, Ladefoged's example demonstrates that only two or three syllables and/or boundary pulses ever occur between the ictuses (I added two ictuses in brackets that he omitted), and that often the ictus occurs on the pulse of the boundary (as it did in our chant examples above). Whereas Ladefoged used stress marks before the syllables, I use the ictus mark below the vowel in order to emphasize the likeness to the chant method.

Stresses in English tend to recur at regular intervals of time. It is perfectly

possible to tap on the stresses in time with a metronome. The rhythm can even

be said to determine the length of the pause between phrases. An extra tap can be

put in the silence, as shown by the marks within the parentheses. (p. 102)

What Ladefoged has done in this illustration is measure the language. Within lengths of utterance the primary rhythm (the foot) becomes simply a unit of measurement—the rational measure—which always begins with the ictus and includes the one or two unstressed pulses grouped with it before the recurrence of another ictus. Ladefoged does not say that the measure will be limited to three such pulses, and his text does not indicate that he recognizes this fact. But his practice indicates that measurement will finally produce the smallest units. The smallest rhythmic units (as Lehiste also explains) will never be less than two pulses. Nor will it be more than three pulses, since as soon as four occur, they will break into two-plus-two.

All modern musical measures, although usually written in bars of larger groupings ($\frac{4}{4}$) ($\frac{6}{8}$), are broken down by the performer into their little measures: $\frac{4}{4}$ is $2 + 2$; $\frac{6}{8}$ is $3 + 3$ or, occasionally, $2 + 2 + 2$; and the uneven bars of some contemporary music, such as $\frac{15}{8}$, will be broken into a mixed group of 2s and 3s, perhaps $3 + 3 + 3 + 2 + 2 + 2$, which may appear unlikely to the musical layman, but is precisely how the first two phrases of the *Spiritus Domini* would appear if barred into modern music and preceded by an upbeat.

These long, mixed binary and ternary units are identical to those we find in OE verses (half-lines). That is why the terminology of "feet" (as used by Sievers) creates confusion. And speaking of *members* can do the same unless we understand how a *member* can be either a measure or only one of the pulses in a measure.

The terminology of measures clarifies this confusion, not because a measure is like a foot, but because it is *not* like a foot. This distinction is important. A *foot* describes a simple rhythm, both its shape (iambic: upbeat-downbeat; trochaic: downbeat-upbeat, etc.) and its length (anapestic: two pulses of upbeat and one downbeat; etc.). A *measure* always begins with the downbeat and includes the one *or* two upbeat pulses that follow it before the next downbeat. Hence, measure is a rational segment of a continuing movement from ictus to ictus; it is an interval of time always extending from one ictus to the next. One should not speak of one measure as a primary rhythm (as we did above of poetic feet). When we speak of measures, we assume a sequence or succession of them, linked one to the next like inches in a ruler.

To go a step further: describing a line as iambic pentameter is giving something of a rhythmic description, whereas describing it as five measures long says nothing at all about the rhythm of that line, except in terms of downbeats and upbeats, which is something closer to timing than to rhythm proper. The use of the terms iambic and trochaic to describe the rhythm of lines or of whole works is an expanded use of these words, of course, but one that seems perfectly legitimate, even though the terms may do no more than indicate whether line units begin with the stressed or the unstressed syllable. But when lines flow from one to the next with seeming disregard of such regularity, the terms not only become useless, but the mentality created by their usage presents a host of new difficulties.

The result of one of these difficulties in the nineteenth century was the invention of the term anacrusis for the unstressed syllable at the beginning of an otherwise trochaic line. Meters of a fixed number of feet or members need such a concept. But when rhythm in sound is understood as the synthesis of a continuing flow of auditory material (sounds and pauses, syllables and boundaries), then it follows that sound may enter in at any point of the continuum; hence it can be measured in the analytical process as coming in on the upbeat or the downbeat, both at the beginning of a work or within it.[22] When the pattern of unstressed to stressed sounds is very regular in line units of equal length, we can speak of the whole in terms of the pattern in a single unit, for example as iambic; but when stress to unstress, syllables or boundaries, group themselves into very irregular units, their being linked together is more important than their individuality, since any regularity of pattern will be occurring on a different level than that of simple rhythm.

This is saying no more than the following: since it is impossible to speak of the irregular poetic rhythm in OE and in much contemporary poetry in terms of classical feet because the patterning principle does not occur on that level, it is useful to analyze it in terms of measures; this device reveals the irregularity on this level of the rhythmic process, an irregularity that enhances the complexity of the regularity on the final level, that of rhythmic synthesis.

THE ELEMENT OF SYNTHESIS: COMPOSITE RHYTHM

In their book, *The Rhythmic Structure of Music,* Grosvenor W. Cooper and Leonard B. Meyer describe the function of rhythm as a synthesis in a way that agrees exactly with what the Solesmes scholars demonstrate about this final level of rhythmic analysis:

As a piece of music unfolds, its rhythmic structure is perceived not as a series of discrete independent units strung together in a mechanical, additive way like beads, but as an organic process in which smaller rhythmic motives, while possessing a shape and structure of their own, also function as integral parts of a larger rhythmic organization.[23]

This larger rhythmic organization is the synthesis, or composite rhythm. When analyzed, it emphasizes the peaks of the rhythmic movement within a continuity rather than the dividing lines of measurement. The dividing lines of measurement were our concern in the preceding section. It is the synthesis, or composite rhythm, that concerns us here.

The example from the *Spiritus Domini* with which we opened this chapter did not illustrate the composite rhythm in any visually graphic way. We can do so now by tracing over it a pattern of *chironomy,* the Greek word for "hand rule." Chironomy describes a conductor's hand motions, which may include the mixture of unequal times (binary and ternary measures) without distorting the movement. Usually, the chant conductor in performance will, as in modern music, indicate the composite rhythm rather than each compound beat; nevertheless, a chironomy tracing which recognizes each measure shows something of the integrity of each longer (three pulses) or shorter (two pulses) measure:

SPIRI - TUS Domi - ni + reple - vit orbem ter - ra-rum,

On the other hand, in illustrating the final rhythmic synthesis (composite rhythm) of this work, we would probably change the tracing to the following:

SPIRI - TUS Domi - ni ∗ reple - vit orbem ter - ra-rum,

In so tracing the chironomy we are recognizing the combination of linguistic and melodic features present in and over the Latin long syllables: *-ri-* of *Spiritus, -ple-* of *replevit,* and *or-* of *orbem,* all of which are ornamented with rising neums. The rest of the syllables and neums are gathered up, so to speak, to fill out the rises and falls of these three rhythmic peaks in the phrase, although they measure out to be eighteen measures with forty-two simple pulses.[24]

The rising neums over the three syllables noted above are characteristic of the handling of the rhythmic high points in chant, those points which create the composite rhythm—the rhythmic synthesis of the otherwise rhythmically loose material. This is true of the syllabic chant of both psalmody and lessons as well as of neumatic chant. The prototype for this is provided by psalm tones. For example, the one given on page 37 shows a rising intonation at the beginning which puts the first important syllable on the recitation tone, another lift at the caesura, and another intonation pattern at the end which emphasizes the last important syllable and then brings the voice down to rest again.

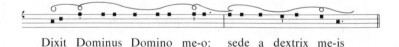

Dixit   Dominus   Domino   me-o: sede   a   dextrix   me-is

Neumatic chant simply ornaments these three points with additional notes. Depending on the importance of the whole text and its use in the liturgy it may also pick up other important words to ornament. As an example of this last statement, the reader might notice in the Spiritus Domini above the melodic ornamentation over *-mi-* of *Domini,* and *-le-* of *alleluia.* The handling of the rising neums is less dramatic, but there is certainly some emphasis, as there is also in the drop and return (doh-sol-doh) over *terrarum.*

Anyone who has studied prominence and intonation patterns in spoken language has already guessed the analogy I am about to draw. The psalm tones are formalized melodic patterns of the intonation contours of speech, and especially of what occurs when a speaker without electronic amplification projects his voice in declamation.[25] As we saw in the preceding section, such contours are sometimes called sentence-level stress—the one or more syllables from the numerous ictuses in a sentence that will be heard as stressed.[26] If only one is heard, it will normally be the final ictus to occur in conjunction with the sentence-termination boundary. Although usually thought of as a stress (primary stress, stress peak) this ictus will normally include the prosodic features of pitch and duration as well (intensity, frequency, and length). Hence, Lehiste calls it *phonological prominence*. This prominence provides the composite rhythm in the flow of English speech.

I call the ictus which bears phonological prominence a *phrase stress*. The term is descriptive in that the prosodic feature of stress (and whatever that may include) is present and occurs on the phonological level in conjunction with some kind of phrasal boundary. The term is also useful because it does not limit. Practically any word in an utterance can receive phrase stress either because of the speaker's intention (emphasis or contrast) or because of linguistic, syntactic, and phonological structures built into the phrases and sentences—for example, parallel structure, use of alliteration and other sound likenesses, and the expectation and repetition of patterns of alternation set up in like units such as verses of poetry.

SUMMARY

The chant masters of the Solesmes school have described the rhythm of Gregorian Chant as sounds grouped in time by means of an ictus into measures of two and three pulses which are in turn gathered up into the one or two rhythmic syntheses marking a melodic and/or linguistic phrase.

Applying the principles of chant rhythm, I have suggested that in the language medium of poetry the sounds are both syllables and the pulses of word- and phrase-boundaries which are grouped into little measures of two and three pulses by an *ictus*. This ictus is a word-level stress which has the capacity of bearing sentence-level stress (prominence) when words are strung together into phrases and sentences, although at times only one such ictus may be perceptible in a sentence. The one or more points of prominence in a phrase (I call this the *phrase stress*) may be created either by the natural phonological system of one to a phrase or by the intention of the speaker or performer to provide emphasis or contrast. Phrase stresses create the composite rhythm in the flow of English speech and hence must always be part of prosodic analysis.

3 APPLYING THE METHOD
TO BEOWULF

_I_n this chapter I will apply the method I have just devised from a combination of Gregorian Chant and linguistic theories to OE poetry, specifically to _Beowulf_. In doing so I will partially invert the order established in chapter 2 and begin with a description of the composite rhythm, since the metrical pattern derives from it, and follow that with some details of the OE material of rhythm before demonstrating the measurement.

COMPOSITE RHYTHM AS THE METER OF _BEOWULF_

In OE poetry, the meter is patterned by the phrase stresses, hence, by the elements of the synthesizing rhythm of speech. This pattern is more complex, however, than appears when it is described as two strong stresses to a half-line. The pattern of rhythmic alternation which gives each phrasal verse two positions of prominence (rhythmically, two arses, or downbeats) also require two positions of contrasting unstress (two theses, or upbeats). Thus, OE meter is better described as a pattern of two phrase stresses in verses (short, phrasal lines) of four positions (members).[1] This is the basic metrical unit of OE poetry found in every instance in the manuscript of _Beowulf_. It is present as an abstract pattern—sometimes realized in less successful poetry and sometimes in highly imaginative and successfully complex metrical expressions—even when the rhythm of the language in its concrete expression deviates from it, which it will do in as many ways as the pattern itself can tolerate.

One remove from, but nevertheless part of, the traditional meter in OE poetry is the pattern of linking two verses into long lines by means of alliteration on certain of the phrase stresses. On this level of patterning, variation is something of a requirement; the rule apparently called for three (aa | ax) or two (ax | ax) (xa | ax) of the four phrase stresses in a long line to alliterate. However, the fact that in some lines all four alliterate —usually in crossed patterns (ab | ba, ab | ab), but in a few instances all together (aaaa)—is proof that the principle of variation is built into this level of patterning. That means that the *pattern* cannot be written in one abstract formula; we used six here, and other patterns are attested to in the *Beowulf* manuscript.

Even on its first level of patterning—four member verses with two phrase stresses—it is not possible to write only one abstract formula. Once we begin to position the two phrase stresses in a verse of four members (x x x x), we need at least five: the Five Types of Sievers, (x́ x x́ x), (x x́ x x́), (x x́ x́ x), (x́ x́ x x), (x́ x x x́). And I propose that we need a sixth (x x x́ x́) which may have evolved later in time, beginning in verses with extended linguistic material and then used in the shorter verses when inflected endings began to be lost and words contracted.

The point I am making about the regularity and irregularity of an abstract pattern is not facetious. It illustrates something about the character of the metrical principle operating in OE poetry (like the principle operating in contemporary free verse) as different from the metrical principle operating in English poetry using classical feet. The dominating meter in the latter tradition, the iambic pentameter, has one abstract pattern: five ictus positions alternating with five unstressed positions: x x́ x x́ x x́ x x́ x x́. Even when classical feet are not patterned, when it is only the number of ictuses or the number of syllables that forms the pattern, it is possible to write it in one abstract formula: for example, Coleridge's *Christabel:* ' ' ' '; and Dylan Thomas' "In My Craft or Sullen Art": x x x x x x x. But this is never possible for OE meter.

It seems to me that the difference follows from the essential character of the unit (the line) which carries the pattern. Since the OE unit (the verse, short line) is essentially a linguistic phrase—the pattern in it is created by phrase stresses—its shape is determined by syntax and semantics; and the pattern of phrase stresses will shift within the units according to the phrasal structure and meaning. In the other tradition, the essential character of the line-unit is that it contain a certain number of ictuses—those points of potential stress which occur on every second or third pulse in all English language utterances. The number of ictuses can thus determine a line regardless of where syntactic and semantic phrases begin and end.

This kind of theorizing leads us to the next step in prosodic analysis. Since the elements creating the metrical patterns in one tradition are always present in the language and therefore present and operating in the verses of the other tradition, those elements *not* abstracted for the pattern are the ones which create the rhythmical variations in a given meter. For example, in iambic pentameter verses, variation is provided by syntactic and semantic phrasing which causes enjambment or run-on lines and caesuras, as well as the prominence of a varied number of phrase stresses among the five ictuses and sometimes in unstressed positions. In OE verses, on the other hand, variation is provided by the number of ictuses (in addition to the two which become phrase stresses) and the number and character of unstressed pulses between them; and this has to do with how the four members (positions) in a verse are realized—whether as single syllables, or by becoming full measures, or by the syllables being replaced by the pulses of word boundaries.

We find the abstract pattern of OE meter realized in the concrete language of *Beowulf* in such varied verses as the following succession:[2]

```
1750: fædde    béagas  # 7he  þa  fórð   ge  scéaft  |
       1    2     1      231 2  1   2      1    2     1    2


       for  gýteð   7for   gýmeð  |  þæs  þe  him  ær
        3    1 3     1 2    1 2  3   1    2   1    2


       gód  +  séalde  |
        1   2    1    2  3
```

In the first of these, the abstract pattern is easily distinguished since the verse has exactly four syllables to fill its four members (x́ x x́ x). In the succeeding verses the four members may be increasingly difficult to ascertain, because the verses contain six and seven syllables. Obviously then, if there are always four members, member means something other than a certain number of syllables.

As we saw in chapter 1, Kaluza offered something of a generative model concerning the four-member verses, and Cable is the most recent prosodist to present a restatement of this theory. Using the terminology I have drawn from Gregorian Chant rhythm in chapter 2, and in an effort to set up a methodology for analyzing the verses of *Beowulf,* I offer the following refinement of the four-member model.

A GENERATIVE MODEL OF THE FOUR-MEMBER THEORY

The basic pattern of an OE verse appears in the abstract as four beats (x x x x). The best example of *potential variation* in this pattern may be discovered in a verse like 1881a: *guð rinc gold wlanc,* which may be performed as either x́ x̀ x́ x̀ or x́ x̆ x́ x̆, or even x́ x́ x́ x́. The law of rhythmic alternation, which rules that two primary stresses cannot be juxtaposed, will cause one of two things to happen.[3] Either two of the syllables will be reduced and the other two heightened, or if all four receive primary stress additional pulses of time will be interposed between them.

The two alternatives provide the model for all of the verses in *Beowulf*, but it is the second which gives us the generating principle. That principle holds that any of the four members may either be a single syllable or generate a measure (which may be a single beat or a compound beat-measure). Thus, *gúð rínc góld wlánc* is really a pattern of x+ x+ x+ x+, in which the + symbol represents the pulse of time required in the word boundaries to allow each syllable to be emphasized. Although in the OE realization of the four members there are never four phrase stresses in a verse, that potential remains, operating to generate additional measures, as in 346b: *gif he us ge un nan wile* (xx xx x́x x́x).

On the other hand, the first alternative is the one which provides the requirement that in a four-member verse there will be only two *phrase stresses*. By heightening two of these members and reducing the other two the four members constitute only two measures (x́ x x́ x). However,
$$1 \quad 2 \quad 1 \quad 2$$
any one of the members may be extended by another syllable (or boundary pulse) and still remain two measures, in this case a ternary measure. For example: 5a: *monegum mægþum* (x́x x x́ x), and 8a: *weox under wolcnum* (x́ xx x́ x).

Our examples thus far all show the two phrase stresses in the same positions, Sievers' type A. We know, however, that they may occur on any two of the members, as in the following: 507a: *onsidne sæ* (x x́ x x́), and 105a: *won sæli wer* (x́ x̀ x x́).[4] But something else shows up in the measurement of these two verses that is not usually apparent and that bears on the four-member theory. In order to complete the measurement we must include the pulses provided in the line breaks, thus: 507a: | *on s í d n e   s ǽ* | and 105a: *wón s ǽ l i   wér* |, and there are
$$1 \quad 2 \quad 1 \quad 2 \quad 1 \quad 2 \qquad\qquad 1 \quad 2 \quad 3 \quad 1 \quad 2$$
always five or six pulses in such types of verses as a result of the preceding and/or following line-break pulses being included. On the other hand, if the two phrase stresses are juxtaposed and neither accepts reduction, they force a line-internal word-boundary pulse to intervene between them as in the following: 57a: *heah healf dene* (x́+ x́ x̀ x), and 4a: *Oft scyld*
$$12 \quad 1 \quad 2 \quad 3$$
scefing (| x x́+ x́ x), thus producing five or six pulses though main-
$$1 \quad 2 \quad 12 \quad 1 \quad 2$$
taining four members. As in these examples, I will always include the bar-symbol for the line-break pulse or pulses (|) (||) as well as the + for the line-internal word-boundary pulse whenever it is part of the measurement of a verse.

The word-boundary pulses between two juxtaposed phrase stresses, on the other hand, may be replaced by unstressed syllables: 21a:

fromum feoh giftum (x́x x́ x̀ x) or 106b: *for scrifen hæfde*
$\qquad\qquad\qquad$ 12 1 2 3

(| x x́x x́ x). Or, as we saw above, additional unstressed syllables
1 2 12 1 2

may be added to any one of the original members, as in 346b: *gif he us ge un nan wile* (xx xx x́x x́x).
$\qquad\qquad\qquad\qquad\quad$ 12 12 12 12

The potential for lengthening has been exemplified in the above. Conversely, there is also the potential for lightening and shortening the linguistic material in the verses. With the heightening of the two phrase stresses, the two reduced syllables can, at least theoretically, be reduced to the point of being replaced by boundary pulses, because such pulses are found in other verses. I say theoretically only because this happens rarely in *Beowulf.* But it does happen in such verses as 947a: *secg betsta* (x́ + x́ x) and 3124a: *hilde rinc* (x́ x x́ #). And it finds its ultimate
1 2 1 2 $\qquad\qquad\qquad\qquad$ 1 2 1 23

realization in the unique verse 2488a: *hreas blac* (x́ + x́ |).
$\qquad\qquad\qquad\qquad\qquad\qquad\qquad\quad$ 1 2 1 2

It would be possible from the foregoing hypothesis to formulate the following description of OE meter (or in linguistic terms, to generate the following rule):

Abstract Pattern Rule: OE verses have four members, two of which are
$\quad$ syllables bearing phonological prominence.
Realization Rules:
$\quad$ 1. A member is typically constituted by a syllable.
$\quad$ 2. A syllable in any and all of the member-positions may become a
$\quad\quad$ measure by the addition of another syllable or a boundary pulse.
$\quad$ 3. A syllable in a lesser-stressed member position may be displaced
$\quad\quad$ by the boundary pulse of either a line break or a line-internal
$\quad\quad$ boundary.

And the potential for rhythmical variation provided within this description ranges from the abstract pattern (x́ x x́ x), which can theoretically be realized as x́ + x́ |, to the ultimate length of a theoretical realization xxx xxx xxx xxx, which I do not find in *Beowulf.*

THE OE MATERIAL OF RHYTHM

Before applying the rules we just described in a measurement of the verses of *Beowulf,* we need to recognize some characteristics of the linguistic material in OE to which we will assign pulses of time.[5] Although such pulses will be assigned very specifically as one to a syllable, one to line-internal boundaries (+) and line-break (|) boundaries, and two to line breaks where clause or sentence termination occurs (‖ and #), the time of the pulse is in no way to be considered absolute. It is relative to the amount of linguistic material in the syllable and to the environment in which the boundary as well as the syllable occur. In one instance the time may be minimal, and in another it may seem more like the value of two. By using the relative whole number—chosen for its analogy to the relative quantity of the punctum in chant—we hope to avoid the presumption of assigning specific durational length to English syllables.

OE SYLLABLES[6]

Two qualities of syllables enter into every treatment of OE meter: the duration of long vowels and syllables as distinct from short vowels and syllables, and whether one or two sound-shapes are present in the phonemic circumstances of diphthongs, syllabic consonants, and syllables separated by intervocalic liquids.

Concerning duration, we have sufficient evidence that there was a real distinction in OE between long and short vowels, and between long, closed syllables and short, open ones. But there is no evidence that these should be regarded as having a 2:1 temporal ratio according to the rules for classical prosody,[7] especially in view of the fact that the classical concept of "numbers" was transferred from the 2:1 of longs and shorts to syllables as 1:1 entities under the influence of just such vernacular languages as OE; we saw this in chapter 1 above (p. 14) when discussing Bede's definition of rhythm. I assume that the syllable in OE constituted one metrical pulse (x or *prótos chrónos*) whether it was long or short, but that then the length—which may have been extended sometimes as much for the sake of emphasis, and usually in the prominence of a phrase stress, as it was by its inherent quantity—provided a rhythmical variation to that pulse.

Such an assumption affects, of course, the use of the concept of resolution as a metrical device; but it seems to me that resolution can have real meaning only in a system whose meter is determined by the suprasegmental phoneme of quantity, that is, in a system based on isochronous or proportional units of time where the 2:1 ratio is requisite. Once syllables may take on relative length without affecting the position of phrase stress and/or of metrical ictus,[8] such length has no significance in the metrical pattern, because it will not matter if one of the four members is filled by a single long syllable or by two which constitute a measure. At the same time, the reality of durational differences in OE may have been heard to the extent of suggesting a likeness between two short syllables and one long, which may well account for the poet's frequent use of them in the way the metrists' "rule" of resolution now dictates that he must do.

Manuscript evidence may be used to support this position of giving a count to every syllable if the evidence is taken as peripheral only and not substantial. The spacings within words in this instance seem to indicate something about how the scribe may have heard the phonemes. Usually he spaced between morphic elements, and often he gave both space and letter-size prominence to final sounds or syllables which prosodists have sometimes underdotted or suggested as being no longer heard as a separate sound. For example:

81: sinc æt symle sele hlifa de.
1681: wundor smiþa ge weorc 7þa þas worold ofgeaf.

Such evidence gains some strength from the fact that the OE scribes did reflect in their spelling dialectal variants and also changes occurring in the language in late OE.[9]

There are at least two or three circumstances where scholars have found it difficult to agree on whether one or two sound-shapes are present. These concern diphthongs, syllabic consonants, and syllables separated by intervocalic liquids and the like.

Diphthongs, in the opinion of Daniel Jones, are "indivisible gliding sounds."[10] Quirk and Wrenn modify this only to the extent of saying that "two vowel sounds were heard," although they were pronounced with one crest of sonority, "so that they formed one syllable and not two."[11] There are others who contend that the long diphthongs may have been disyllabic, supporting their conclusion by the fact that in the manuscripts "the long diphthongs do not exhibit the variations in spelling which characterize short diphthongs."[12] Although the issue is far from settled, I assume the diphthong to be monosyllabic, as defined by Quirk and Wrenn, and hence to constitute one beat. In my demonstration, when the monosyllabic diphthong is in a position requiring a second beat, as in the first stress position of C and D type verses, the second beat will be illustrated as being filled by a boundary pulse, even though some readers may pronounce the glide so as seeming to fill both beats with either one lengthened sound or two distinct sound shapes.

On the other hand, I recognize the so-called disyllabic diphthong as something different. For example, *frea*, as descended from the Primitive OE *fræw-ja* (Gothic *frau-ja*), was evidently disyllabic in origin and probably remained so at the time of the compositiion of our poem, in contrast

to *þeod* (compare Gothic *þiuda,* which clearly contains the reflex of
Indo-European Primitive Germanic /ew/ + consonant).

These so-called disyllabic diphthongs are a useful example of how the
OE meter accommodated the changes in language in late OE. Although
such words as *frea, don, seon* may still have been disyllabic when *Beowulf*
was composed, they obviously were not disyllabic when the tenth-century
scribe was recording the poem as he heard it. One must assume that what
he recorded, whether from dictation or from an earlier manuscript,
sounded right to him, and assume also that he was both accustomed to
hearing his native poetry and concerned enough about his transcriptions
being read correctly to insert the generally accepted rhythmic marks of
accents and points. He recorded these words as monosyllables, and I treat
them as such in my measurement and use them to support my hypothesis
of a sixth type. When they occur in the final position in a verse as
monosyllables with stress, they are followed by the line-break pulse which
fills out the measure they began, as in the following:

1116b: | 7 on bǽl + dón #
          12 3   1   2   1   23

2034: þónne he mid   fǽm nan | on   flétt + gǽð. |
        1   2   1   2   1   2   1   2   1   2   1   2

When there was still a second syllable, and when it was still pronounced in
archaic practice in the tenth century, it simply added another count to the
measure. Those who prefer, on the other hand, to read these words as
always disyllabic may simply replace the boundary with the second
syllable, as in the following:

839: fér don   fólc+togan | féor ran 7néan |
       1   2   1 2 1 2 3   1   2   3 1 2

                                    nea[ha]n |
                                      1   2 3

Syllabic consonants and syllables dependent on liquids and nasals
require somewhat more individual treatment, and this may be noted in the
instances which occur in the lines used in the following pages. In general,
however, the same rule which in Modern English divides final consonant
clusters such as [cand + le] and [rhyth + m] I assume to be operating in
such OE words as [maþ + m] and [bearht + m], especially when these are
found elsewhere in the manuscript preceded by unstressed vowels.[13] This
view obviously regards as having two syllables such words as *dohtor* and

morðor (which Bliss underdots, it seems to me, far too freely in order to force all the lines into the subtypes he permits[14]), and also makes [wo + rold] two sound shapes (stretches of sound over which stress extends). My treatment of such words as constituting two relative pulses, however, does not mean to imply two equally stressed syllables; it indicates only a simple rhythm, the upbeat of which in some recitations is so light as to be constituted as much by a boundary as by distinct or separate sound. The lightest variety is exemplified in line 1763:

		(+)					
þæt	þec	adl	oððe	ecg |	eafoþes		ge twæfeð |
1	2	1 2	1 2	1 2	1 2 1		2 1 2 3

Disyllabic diphthongs, syllabic consonants, and syllables dependent on intervocalic liquids, then, demand some discrimination when handling OE syllables as the material of OE poetry. But the general rule still applies: in scanning, every syllable either is simply counted or is represented in the abstract by the symbol *x*, which designates one pulse of time relative to the phonemic requirements of the sound shape it represents. It may be lengthened up to, but not become, two counts; or it may be as short as possible without, however, losing its value as a separate sound shape.

BOUNDARIES IN OE

Much has already been made of the significance of the time heard in line breaks and in line-internal boundaries, and the latter have been assigned time in chapter 2 corresponding roughly to the phrasing bars found in Gregorian Chant. I assume that such boundaries occurred in OE as they do in present-day English speech, and that such intervals must have been heard clearly in the breaks between the short, phrasal verses, and patterned into the meter, because the verse units have been recognized from the beginnings of modern scholarship on *Beowulf*. The OE scribes also provided clues in the manuscript to their recognition with points, which probably invite less danger when used for prosodic interpretations than do the accents and spacings.[15]

The points are used only sporadically by the scribes. In the *Beowulf* manuscript of 3182 long lines there are some seven hundred points.[16] Over six hundred occur at the end of long lines, and some sixty at the end of the first verse. This statistic supports the view that the OE poet and the listener heard the verses linked into long lines; hence, long lines are distinctively metrical units. But the verse is the first unit, and sufficient points occur after verse units to give additional support to their function as metrical units. For this reason I never call the break between the verses of a long line a *caesura*. Caesuras, historically from the Greek, signify a syntactic and semantic phrasal break within a line unit, and the term is used in this way when applied to English poetry written in the tradition of classical feet. The use of the term to refer to the break for the constant short-line unit in OE poetry has thus created unwarranted confusion. I consider the short line (verse) to be the fundamental metrical unit in OE poetry and the linking of two such verses to be somewhat analogous to the linking of two lines of iambic pentameter by means of rhyme in the heroic couplet.

Hence, I always count one (|) or two (||, #) pulses of time in the breaks between the short lines (the verses) as well as between long lines, and the amount of time depends on syntax and semantics. I am not the first to do so, of course. John C. Pope made much of the initial rest (the harp stroke) which he posited at the beginning of type B and type C verses demanding something additional before the first stress. He also uses pulses other than syllables (following Heusler and Kaluza) in other places, for example when the last count of a verse is a quarter note or a quarter or eighth rest (see his pp. 164–65, lines 1, 2, 14, and 16). On the other hand, no allowance has been made for the boundary pulse between the verses in lines 3, 4, 15, and 20. Pope does recognize additional time between the verses in line 11, and a complete stop at the end, but he gives this the sign of an indefinite pause (⌢).

Line breaks take time and so are part of the material of rhythm. As such, they are part of the continuing movement and timing of the language and not breaks in the measurement. Those that take only one pulse of time (|) are always part of measures which also contain syllables. In most of the cases where two-pulse breaks (|| and #) occur—wherever ordinary punctuation would demand a period, colon, or dash, question or exclamation mark, and usually also a semicolon—they are also part of the surrounding measures. The following example from *Beowulf* illustrates all three types of line breaks:

```
658:  háfa     nu    7ge   héald |  húsa    sélest  ||
       1 2      1    2 3     1      2   1   2    1 2   31

      ge mýne       mǽrþo |  mǽgen   ellen   cýð |
       2   1 2       1   2 3   1 2     1  2     1  2

      wáca    wið   wráþum. # ne   bið þe   wílna   gád |
       1 2     3     1 2   3 1 2    1   2    1   2    1 2

               (or: wráþum. # ne    bið   þe )
                     1 2 1 2  1      2     3

      gif þu þæt   éllen   wéorc |  áldre ge dígest #
       3   1  2     1  2     1     2 1  2   3  1 2   12
```

In every case except the final one, the pulse is counted in measures which contain syllables. The ictus of a new measure often begins in a break, as in lines 658 and 660. These cases will nearly always coincide with Pope's use of the initial rest; what Pope does not do, of course, is consistently allow for that beat at every verse break.

Whether the two-pulse line breaks are part of surrounding measures or constitute measures by themselves depends entirely on the arrangement of the surrounding stressed and unstressed syllables. When a verse ends with a stressed syllable, the pulses of the break will always complete the measure begun by that stressed syllable (as in 658a, 659b, 660b, and 661a above). When a verse begins with one unstressed syllable before a stressed syllable (as 659a above), the new measure will always begin in the preceding break. Or it may have begun in the preceding verse and simply include the pulse of the break. The following lines show this happening twice, between 510b and 511a, and then within 511:

```
510: áldrum   néþdon ‖ ne   inc   ænig   món |
      1    2   1 2 3 1 2   3   1  2    1   2

     neléof  ne  láð | be  léan +míhte |
      3   1   2   1   2  3    1 2  1  2 3
```

But the two-pulse line break may also constitute a measure by itself, as it does in line 661 of the four-line example preceding the above. And I have scanned it to do so in some 650 lines of *Beowulf*. I always give it only two pulses, although it could have three. These measures do not break the rhythm; they are necessary for the movement of time natural to the syntax. And when the poet interjects a statement that constitutes a verse line by itself, perhaps a dramatic apostrophe or bit of gnomic advice, the two-pulse breaks surrounding it may account for two entire measures, as in the following:

```
343: béod   ge néatas ‖ béowulf   is   min náma #
      1     2  1 2 1 2 1  2     1    2   1 212
```

However, in my scansion of *Beowulf* two such full measure breaks stand alone in only ten lines. In all of the others they include syllabic material of the surrounding verses.

Because I introduced the points in the *Beowulf* manuscript above to give additional support to the reading of pulses of time between verses, I must also recognize the fact that thirteen of the points are actually found within the verses. These I read as the scribe's hearing the same kind of time-consuming boundary that he heard occurring between verses. Most of these coincide with the usual placement of a caesura (and here the term is used accurately), especially by Bliss. I do not find it necessary to supply an additional pulse in all these instances; however, where these thirteen line-internal points occur the phrasing would be heightened by a boundary pulse, and this must be what the scribe heard as he was writing, for example, in line 61: *heoro gar* · *7hroð gar 7halga til.* He must have heard a phrase boundary taking a silent pulse and perhaps confused it with the line break. On the other hand, he may not have been confused at all but may simply have wanted to alert the reader to provide the rhythmic lengthening necessary at these points for proper phrasing and a clear and forceful reading, as in line 2673b: *byrne·* *nemeahte.*

The above are phrase boundaries, and I recognize fewer of them within verses requiring an additional pulse when I count measures. However, I always recognize the additional pulse required for the word boundary when the two phrase stresses are juxtaposed, as was pointed out earlier. For both of these situations I assign one pulse and use the plus symbol (+) to distinguish them from line breaks.

There are some other instances when the measurement demands an upbeat so that a new measure can begin. Most often this will occur between a phrase stress and an intermediate stress (as found in Sievers types D and C). However, other circumstances have to be present before a boundary pulse will intervene. For example, the following a-verses are metrically identical, but their performance may differ depending on the interpretation of the line break in line 31, where the syntax calls for no more than one pulse but the b-verse begins on the downbeat. I include two interpretations:

```
31: léof + lánd + frùma  |  lánge   áhte  #
     1    2   1    2   1 2 3   1    2    1   2 3 1

  [or] léof + lánd   frùma ‖  lánge   áhte  #
        1    2   1        2 3 1 2  1    2    1 2   3 1

57: héah + héalf   dène ‖ héold  þenden   líf de  |
     1    2   1       2 3 1 2  1      2    3      1    2 3
```

If the second interpretation of line 31 is used, giving extra time in the break, the syntax would be marked by a different intonational contour from that used in line 57. Since this kind of rhythmical nuance occurs all the time in modern English speech, there is no reason to doubt that it would have occurred in the formal recitation of OE poetry, especially since the measurement shows one choice or another necessary in line 31.

On the other hand, a theory of overstressing in OE poetry would usually start a new measure with such secondary stresses as we have in types E and D, and hence interject such boundary pulses freely. My own reading, therefore, is always conservative in the use of the line-internal boundary pulse. I use it in cases like the above only when the rhythmic material following seems to call for it, and when its use is further supported by such manuscript evidence as spacing, an accent on the preceding syllable, or an oddly placed point. I am attempting to provide as far as possible a measurement of the OE material that is visually attested, and not a description of a single performance.

In demonstrating the material of rhythm in OE (syllables and boundary pulses) we have already been including the entire measurement process because it was impossible to do otherwise and still show how syllables and pulses move in time.

THE OE RATIONAL MEASURE

Measures, as chapter 2 demonstrated, are a product of rational analysis. They are the smallest possible units within a rhythmic interval of language. They always begin with an ictus or downbeat and extend to the next one, never comprising more than two or three pulses of time. Usually the ictus occurs on a syllable capable of bearing stress, but it may also occur within a boundary, as we saw in the previous section. Assigning the ictus position is not difficult in most cases, since we always begin with the two phrase stresses in the verse. In the following long line, for example, I would begin as shown:

772:

wið hæfde héaþo deorum | þæt he on hrús an neféol |
  1 2 1 2   1 2   3 1 2

But there is much material left over after the measures initiated by the phrase stresses have been counted off. The next step is to look for a secondary or intermediate stress, and there is one present in *deorum*. After that it is a matter of choosing the relatively strongest of the normally weak stresses, and in this process much will depend on the context.

In making choices among such unstressed material, as well as in distinguishing between phrase stresses and syllables bearing intermediate stress, I use the rule which Cable stated in his book as a condition: "A syllable can bear metrical ictus only if it has a greater linguistic prominence than at least one adjacent syllable" (*MM* 27). But Cable's use of the word *ictus* is more limited than mine. He uses the term to refer only to the two phrase stresses of all verses, and to the one intermediate stress found in types D and E—that is, to the two or three stresses that are part of the meter of the Five Types. The difference in my usage is important, since my work will generally be read in light of Cable's work which anticipated mine in print. On the other hand, I find his arguments and his presentation of linguistic evidence regarding stress sufficiently convincing to require no repetition of the evidence here.[17] However, Cable does not go beyond the patterns of the Five Types, and thus he has no need to distinguish the ictuses that initiate extra measures. In other words, my purpose is different from his in that my concern is to measure all the material in the verses and long lines in order to reveal information that goes beyond what has been learned from analyses either starting from and arriving again at the Five Types or starting from an assumption of equal measures.

Nevertheless, something of the same condition as that stated by Cable also works for recognizing the syllable or boundary pulse that takes the ictus to initiate the extra measures when verses are extended. And although that syllable may bear no more perceptible stress or prominence than those around it in an ordinary recitation of the verse, it has the capacity to bear stress by reason of syntax or emphasis, that is, if the verse were so chanted as to allow all the little measures to surface. But they will probably never do so because the meter of the poetry is designed to give prominence to two phrase stresses in a verse and thus to subordinate any others.

My choice from among the particles and proclitics in the example given is *he:* it receives the ictus, the small "one" placed below it. The measurement of the line is then completed by initiating the other measure on the line break and checking to see how the first pulse of the line worked into the previous measure:

772:

| wið hǽfde héaþo dèorum | þæt he on hrús an neféol |
  1 2   1   2   1 2 1 2 1 2   1 2   1   2 3   1   2

The long line can be described then as being eight measures long, or four-plus-four in the verses (4/4). Most of the measures are binary, but one is ternary.

A long line, whose measurement is closest to the abstract pattern, on the other hand, would be the following:

91: frúm   sceaft   fíra | féor ran   réccan |
      1   2   1 2 3   1   2   1 2 3

This is a four-measure line (2/2), only about half as long as line 772. In line 91 the syllabic material is also very evenly divided between the measures. Of the approximately two hundred lines of *Beowulf* which have only four measures, the syllabic material is seldom so evenly divided. More often there is a mixture of threes and twos using both syllable and boundary material, as in the following:

```
50: múrnènde      mód # mén ne   cúnnon |
     1   2   3     1  23  1   2    1  2  3
```

```
101: fýre ne   frém man |  féond  on hélle ‖
      1  2  3   1   2  3   1    2    1  2  31
```

and in

```
59: ðæm   féower   béarn |  fórð   gerímed |
     3    1   2     1    2   1     2  1 2  1
```

In line 59, *ðæm* completes a measure begun in the previous line's #-break; and the final break begins a new measure completed in the following line.

FIVE-MEASURE LONG LINES

Slightly more than half (51 percent) of the long lines in *Beowulf* have five measures, with the verses patterned two-plus-three (2/3) or three-plus-two (3/2). Slightly more are in the second pattern, as are the following:

```
396: | under hére   gríman |  hróð gar ge   séon ‖
       1  2   3  1  2    1  2  3   1   2   3   1  23
```

```
     lætað  híl de   bòrd |  hér on bídman |
      1  2   1   2   1   2  1   2    1  2  3
```

The handling of *under* in line 396 is arbitrary, depending on how much prominence the reader chooses to give to it. It can, of course, constitute a measure by itself (*under*) leaving the line break to take the third count of

1   2

the previous measure in line 395. However, I chose to underplay the preposition in order to give *here* additional prominence. Other than this, the lines exhibit no problems in measurement.

Somewhat more difficult choices have to be made in other situations when one begins to measure the material of rhythm in OE long lines with all the previous readings by prosodists in view. For example, line 2 of *Beowulf* has the word *cyninga* in a position that demonstrates a frequent occurrence in the poem:

þéod + cýninga | þrým   ge frúnon |
 1   2 1 2 1 2   1   2   1 2   3

Because the *-ing-* of *cyning* was originally a patronymic, it bears stronger stress than does the inflection *-a*. The question is how to distribute two little measures across the four pulses from *cyn-* through the break. This is probably the kind of situation that causes many prosodists to scan four- and five-pulse feet and measures. However, doing so is only ignoring the issue. The additional ictus will still be present, for a four-beat measure always carries a potential stress on the third beat, thus breaking the four into two-plus-two.

However, this is not the only way in which such a situation can be analyzed. In most speech, and hence in a simple recitation of these lines, the human speech apparatus would provide other solutions. If the performance is one of ordinary reading (as in the classroom for translation purposes), the line break would not be given any time, and the reading might be as follows:

þéod + cýninga   þrým ge frúnon |
 1   2 1 2   3   1   2   1 2   3

A more formal recitation, on the other hand, would put the extra time in the line break, so that *cyninga* would fill one measure:

þéod + cýninga ‖ þrým   ge frúnon |
 1   2 1 2   3 1 2   1   2   1 2   3

My own reading is usually somewhere between these two, depending on the formality of the occasion. But when we turn to the performance of an OE scop we have another consideration, for most scholars now agree that the scop sang the poetry and used a harp for accompaniment. The experience of others now researching the surviving oral literature in Africa offers new evidence to support a theory that oral poets give a very stylized performance. (Indeed, both Pope's analysis and certainly Cable's melodic proposal demand such stylization.) My first reading of the line, assigning the ictus to the third syllable of *cyninga*, fits that kind of stylization. This is identical to Pope's reading of the two little measures since he puts them into one measure of $\frac{4}{8}$ time:

$$| \bar{\char32}\hspace-0.5em\flat\;\; | \;\flat\flat\;\bar{\char32}\hspace-0.5em\flat\; |$$

þeod cýninga
   1 2 1 2

Cable does not consider time or rhythm in this way, but his melodic pattern supplies the vocal nuance necessary to retain the intermediate stress on the second syllable while giving the ictus to the third. If I provide chant notation with rhythmic marks to Cable's melodic reading we have the following:

þeod cyninga þrym ge frunon

Bliss, on the other hand, does not touch on the problem because he does not recognize secondary stress in verses of this type, nor does he read rhythmically from verse to verse.

There are many verses similar in this regard to line 2. When necessary I will assign the ictus to the final syllable as in my first fully measured example, thus assuming a stylized performance by an OE scop.[18] But this will be unnecessary in many situations with this type of three-syllable word coming last in a verse, because the following line break or the beginning of the next verse will allow the third syllable to complete the measure, as in the following:

58b: g l æ d e s c ý l d i n g a s #
     1 2   1 2 3 12

On the other hand, words of this kind may be forced to bear both of the phrase stresses[19] of the meter. Usually when they do, the manuscript provides spacing between the morphemes, though not always and not in the following:

              +
461a: | m i d w í l f í n g u m ‖
     1   2   1 2 1 2   12

But when this is the case, since the meter calls for it, I find no problem in interjecting the (+) pulse and beginning a new measure. Sometimes it is harder to do so between a phrase stress and a secondary stress. Nevertheless, when the secondary stress is a strong second element of a compound around which the scribe spaces clearly, there is again no problem.

We saw an example of this and two ways to handle it in lines 31 and 57 given above at the end of the section on boundaries. Here are two others:

```
427: brégo   béorht + dèna  |  bíddan wílle  |
       1 2      1     2 1 2 3   1  2    1  2 3

742: bát + bán + lòcan  |  blód + édrum   drànc  |
       1 2   1 2   1 2   3    1  2 1   2       1   2
```

The passage in *Beowulf* from which line 742 is taken illustrates many of the points just made. It describes Grendel's devouring of Hondscio, and the lines are short and forceful. Nevertheless, they range in length from four measures to six measures as noted in the right hand margin.

```
739: né þæt   se    áglæca  |  ýl dan    þóhte  |        3/2
       1  2     3   1  2 1 2 1   2       1  2 3
                      +
               or: áglæca  |

740: ac hege   féng + hráðe  |  fór mon   síðe  |        3/2
       1   2 3   1     2   1 2 3  1   2    1 2 3

741: slæpendne   rínc  |  slát + ún  wèarnum  |        2/3
       1 2    3    1     2   1   2 1   2    1  2

742: bát + bán + lòcan  |  blód + édrum   drànc  |      3/3
       1 2   1 2   1 2   3    1  2 1   2       1   2

743: sýn + snædum   swéalh ‖ sóna hæfde  |             3/2
       1 2    1 2      1    23  1 2   1 2 3

744: ún + lýfigendas  |  éal ge  féormod .   |         3/2
       1 2  1 2 1  2  3 1   2  1    2    3

745: fét   7fólma  #  fórð + nèar   æt  stóp  |        2(1)/3
       1    2 1 2    12 1     2  1    2    1  2
```

The last figure in the right hand column was written differently, with the full measure of the line break given in parentheses. I will always indicate this "extra" measure in this way, so that the reader can judge how its inclusion affects my statistics. As may be noted also in lines 743 and 745, I read the type E verses with overstressing, giving the intermediate stress a new ictus as the passage seems to demand. The same could be done in 741b.

SIX-MEASURE LONG LINES

Long lines with six measures are next in frequency to those with five, governing some 35 percent of *Beowulf*. The most frequent pattern is 3/3 (75 percent), shown in the following lines from the passage describing the melting of the giant sword:

```
1605:                        þa þæt    swéord   ongán |
                              1   2        1      2   1   2

         æf t e r    héa þo    swáte |  hílde    gí  c  e lum |
         1     2      1    2    1 2 3   1    2     1     2 1   2

         wíg  bil   wánian # þæt   wæs   wúndra    súm |
          1    2    1   23 12  1     2     1    2    1   2
```

```
1610:  |onwíndeð    wǽl    ràpas |  sege   wéald + háfað |
        12   1   2     1     2 3  1  2 3   1    2   1 2  3
```

However, it seldom occurs in so many successive long lines.

Six measures in a long line are also found in verse combinations of 2/4 and 4/2, but the verse with four measures goes a step beyond a simple mixing of twos and threes. Four, in the terminology of little measures, is two-plus-two. Hence, in the abstract at least, a 2/4 long line is $2 + 2 + 2$. In the combinations forming six measures to a long line, however, these four-measure verses are not really very heavy, as the following show:

```
181: dǽda    démend |  ne wiston   hie   dríhten    gód |
      1 2      1 2    1    2  1   2    3     1    2     1  2

ne   hie    huru   héo  fena    hélm |  hérian    ne   cúþon |
 1     2    1 2     1    2 3     1    2   1   2      3   1 2  3
```

And we often find them in this kind of arrangement—short a-verse, long b-verse, followed by the reverse. Nevertheless, long lines of this type give us in a minimal amount of material a hint of three verses, even though metrically the material is still strictly controlled by the two phrase stresses in two verses. Again, the irregular element in the meter, the alliteration, has already prefigured this new kind of irregularity in measures by its patterns of double-cross alliteration, or four alliterating syllables in patterns of two-plus-two.

I find only two verses in all of *Beowulf* that contain ten syllables, and one of these forms a long line of six measures:

1484:
mæg þonne on þæm gólde ongítan | géa ta drýhten
1 2 3 1 2 1 2 3 1 2 3 1 2 1 2

The other is 1164b, one of the so-called hypermetric lines.

SEVEN- AND EIGHT-MEASURE LONG LINES

Long lines with seven or eight measures will always have complex groupings. In *Beowulf* there is a lower percentage of these expanded lines than in *The Dream of the Rood,* for example; however, some 7 percent of the *Beowulf* lines have seven measures, usually in half-line patterns of 3/4 and 4/3. Sometimes these too, like the 2/4 and 4/2 lines, can be found in successive lines, as shown in the second pair of the following:

684: 3/4
sécge ofer síttan | gif het ge sé cean déar |
1 2 1 2 1 2 1 2 1 2 1 2 1 2

688: 4/3
hýlde hine þa héa þo dèor | hléor + bòlster on féng |
1 2 1 2 3 1 2 1 2 1 2 1 2 3 1 2

1612: 4/3
| ne nóm he in þæm wícum | wéder gèata léod |
1 2 1 2 1 2 1 2 3 1 2 1 2 1 2

3/4
máð m æhta má | þeh he þær mónige ge séah |
1 2 1 2 1 2 1 2 3 1 2 1 2 1 2

Eight-measure long lines constitute less than 1 percent of *Beowulf,* but they are scattered throughout the poem, with more of them outside of the groups classified as hypermetric than within. The pattern in these is normally 4/4, as in the following:

1485: | geséon + súnu hræ̀d les |
1 2 1 2 1 2 1 2 1

þonne he on þæt sínc + státrað 4/4
2 3 1 2 3 1 2 1 2

109: | Nege féah he þære fǽhðe |
1 2 3 1 2 1 2 1 2 3

ac he hine féor for wrǽc | 4/4
1 2 1 2 1 2 1 2

However, both seven- and eight-measure long lines have the possibility of verses with five measures, in patterns of 2/5, 5/2, 3/5, and 5/3, and we have some twenty-one verses in *Beowulf* which can be read in these patterns if I do not refine my distinctions. The refinement is necessary if we are to maintain a theory of four members in the meter of a verse. For as soon as there are five measures, the realization rule—that a member may be a single syllable or it may generate a whole measure—is either broken or inaccurate. The overwhelming number of verses in *Beowulf* that do not exceed the length allowed within the four-member pattern suggest that some refinement may be necessary in the way I measure the long lines.

An examination of the twenty-one verses I read originally with five measures shows them to fall into three categories. Thirteen have a full measure in the line break which closes them;[20] five have an upbeat syllable which completes a measure begun in the preceding line break (usually called an anacrusis);[21] all but one (1545a) of those with anacrusis, and one in addition (1164a), have a three-syllable word in the final position which I had chosen to read as two measures (see pp. 64–65 above) in order to limit the line break to one pulse. One other verse (2367a) presents a unique problem.

The verses in the first category are probably the easiest to reconcile to the four-member pattern, because the fifth measure is composed entirely of the line-break pulse, as in the following b-verses:

1625:   3/4(1)

mǽ g e n	bý r þenne	þara	þe he	him mí d + hǽ f d e #
1 2	1 2	1 2	1 2	1 2	3 1 2 1 2 1 2

2/4(1)

441: dr ý h t n e s	dó m e	s e þe	hine	dé a ð + n í m e ð #
1 2	1 2 3	1 2	1 2	1 2 1 2 1 2

It is probably facile to say that such verses illustrate that the time in the line break should not be counted in a measurement process, just as it is not counted in other types of prosodic analysis such as marking feet or "types." Perhaps this is proof that the verses are separate metrical entities. However, it is the minority of line breaks that do not include some material from the preceding or following verse, and in the full verses of four measures this presents a different kind of problem, as in the following a-verse:

1545:   (?)5/3

# Of sǽ t	þa	þone	sé l e gyst	7hy r e	sé a x e	ge té a h	
1 2	1	2	1 2	1 2 1	2 3 1 2	1 2	3 1 2

This a-verse impinges on both breaks surrounding it. The first syllable of this kind of verse has been written off handily by scholars using the *anacrusis*. But, granting validity to the term, we must probe the rhythmic situation involved in anacrusis if we are to progress in our studies of rhythm in poetry. The handy answer in the previous examples—that the time in the line breaks has nothing to do with the patterns in the verses—is disproved in this one. The time in the line breaks is part of the overall rhythm, and the poet uses it as he pleases, both coming in with syllabic material on the upbeat of a measure begun in the line break and completing a measure across the line break into the following verse, as does this one from the a-verse into the b-verse.

If the four-member theory holds, the poet could apparently use these anacrustic syllables without breaking the pattern, much as we tolerate the eleventh (unstressed) syllable in an iambic pentameter line. In the case of anacrusis, it is the preceding verse ending that is rhythmically involved. Hence, it is an anchronism to say in the case of 1545a that the ictus on the final syllable is compensated by the anacrustic syllable at the beginning. Of course, there is an unstressed syllable at the beginning of the b-verse, and there is also a phrase stress in the final position of 1544, and these are more to the point. For rhythm moves constantly forward in the sound of poetry, as in music, and the oral poetry of the OE was only sound.

The syllabic material in OE poetry is usually connected to the time pulses in the line breaks: I counted only some 650 line breaks that were comprised of full measures within themselves, unconnected to the measured material surrounding them. All the others are part of the preceding or following verse. Many of these Pope has recognized in his measurement of types B and C. Others he accommodates by using quarter notes in the final positions. But a natural line-break pulse he ignores. Hence, his need for theorizing a harp stroke when the ictus occurs in the line break.

It is only in the heavy verses and long lines that these extra syllables and measures involving the line breaks present questions. And we have the real question of a poet's *breaking* the pattern—rather than bending it for the sake of artistic tension—if we assume the OE verses to have a four-member pattern and now find five (member) measures in some verses.

Another group of possible five-measure verses exhibits not only anacrusis, but also a three-syllable word in the final position, as in the following a-verses, which are measured in the manner I described on p. 65 for a chanted performance:

1425:   5/2

#	ge s á won	ð a	æ f t e r	wǽ t e r e		wý rm cȳnne s	f é l a	
1	2 1 2	1	2 3	1 2 1 2		1 2 3	1 2 3	

However, as I suggested in that earlier discussion, a performer could create a different rhythmic nuance by giving extra time in the break, as is usual in ordinary reading. But writing this difference in symbols is confusing, since it requires a double bar in the line break, which otherwise I adopted to signal a marked terminal intonation (questions and exclamations, and some clauses). When I use it in the following reading, it means only a lengthening:

4(1)/2

#	ge s á won	ð a	æf t e r	wǽt e r e	‖ wý rm cỳ nne s	fé l a	
1	2 1 2	1	2 3	1 2 3 12 1	2 3	1 2 3

And in such a reading, the measurement conforms on the basis of not counting the measure in the line break, and also on the basis of not counting the anacrusis. Some other examples like 1425 are the following:

1732:   4(1)/2

	ge	dé ð	h im	swa ge	wé a l	dene	‖ wó ro l de	dǽl a s	
1	2	1	2	1 2	1	2 3 12 1 2 3	1 2 3

1758:   4(1)/2

#be	bé o rh	þe	ð o ne	bé a l o	n i ð	‖ bé owu l f	l é o f a	
1 2	1	2	1 2	1 2	3 12	1 2	1 2 3

However, in these the secondary stress in the final word would be a natural recipient of a new ictus, creating these readings:

wé a l + d è ne		bé a l o	n í ð	
1	2 1 2 3	1 2	1 2

And in this case we would ignore the anacrustic measure and still have four measures in the verse.

If one is tempted to protest that such manipulation is "having it both ways," or "playing both ends against the middle," I would protest that that is precisely what I am doing. More correctly, that is precisely what the poet is doing. I am convinced that this is what a skillful poet always does in the effort to create the tension of rhythmical variations in his given meter. As I repeat to my students: What a poet *can* do, he *may* do. And it is the job of the critic to figure out how he got away with what he did; that is, did he, and how did he, bend the meter as far as possible without breaking it?

One a-verse in *Beowulf* with apparently five measures does not fit any of the above categories for explanation:

2367:   5/3

o f e r   swám ða   s í o l e ð a   b i g o n g | s ú n u   è c g + ð è o w e s |
1 2   1   2   1   2 1   2 1   2   1 2   1   2   1   2   3

Two syllables for anacrusis would be unusual, although *ofer* could be read
as the upbeat of the line-break ictus: # o f e r . On the other hand, since
                                               3 12 3
the b-verse is relatively short, the long line still stays within the limit of
eight measures. Is this another case in which the poet "takes it both ways"?
For we suggested in our first set of five-measure-verse candidates that the
single measure in the line break should not be counted as part of the
four-member pattern. Is verse 2367a then a deviant verse—unmetrical? I
will not answer that question. It cannot be answered until poems like *The
Dream of the Rood* and others characterized by extended verses have been
measured to see if they conform to the four-member pattern as it has been
described.

Perhaps 2367a is a hypermetric verse. In that case, *hypermetric* means
something different from what it has previously been used to mean. Of the
long lines of *Beowulf* that are always grouped as hypermetric, only two are
among the ones we have just discussed: 1164a ends with a three-syllable
word as in our last category; and 1168a shows an accent mark in the
manuscript over *ar*, thus suggesting a word-boundary pulse (a theory I
develop in the essay appended to this study).

A look at all of the so-called hypermetric lines can provide a summary
to the kind of measuring process I have demonstrated in this chapter. And
this is a good place to begin identifying the four members in verses, most
of which in the hypermetric lines will be full measures. In order to
distinguish members I will provide the measurement in an abstract
form—that is, using x's to represent the syllables. What belongs to one
member position (x's, +'s, etc.) will be grouped together. The groupings
will not be consistent with the measures, of course, since a member may be
a single syllable which is part of a measure. In the following hypermetric
passages, for example, where there are fewer than four ictuses in a verse,
one of the four members will be a syllable within a measure—as will be
the case in most verses of average length.

In the right-hand margin the first column gives the number of measures
in each verse, with line-break measures in parentheses. In the second
column is the type of phrase stress pattern I see in each verse. Assigning
types to the verses will lead us into chapter 4 where examples of each of
Sievers' Five Types will be measured. I assign a type label here to the
hypermetric lines—in spite of the fact that most prosodists group them
outside of the Five Type theory—in order to show how measuring the

verses and identifying the four members reveals the pattern that is present. There are instances, of course, when the assignment is somewhat arbitrary, for example in a three measure verse when there is a question of which syllable in one of the measures is the fourth member (ex. 1165a and b, which could be labelled A/F). In these cases I am often guided as much by the previous assignments by prosodists as by any new principle. However, what I see clearly revealed in these extended lines is a sixth type (as in 1164b, 1167, etc.) which I simply call F, and about which I will have more to say in the next chapter.

1163:

x́ xx x́x xx | xx x́x x́ x | 3/3   A/C
1 23 12 12 1 23 12 1 2 3
gán under gýldnum beage | þær þa gódan twégen |

x́x x́xx x̀x x # xxx xx x́x x́xx ‖   3(1)/4(1)   D/F
12 123 12 312 123 12 12 12312
sǽt on súhter ge fǽderan # þagyt wæs hiera síb æt gǽdere ‖

x́x x́x x̀ x # xxx x́x x́ x   3(1)/3   D/C
12 12 1 2 12 123 12 1 2
ǽg hwylc óðrum trỳwe # swyl ce þær hún fer þ þýle

|x x́xx x́+ x̀ xx | xx xxx x́x x́x   4/4   D/F
12 123 12 1 23 1 23 123 12 12
| æt fótum sæt fréan scýl dinga | ge hwylc hiora his férhþe tréow de .

| xx xx x́+ x́x | xx xx x́x x́x | 4/4   F/F
1 23 12 12 12 3 12 12 12 12 3
| þæt he hæf de mód mícel | þeah þe he his mágum nǽre |

1168:

x́+ xx x́xx xx # xx x́x x́ xx ‖   4(1)/3(1)   A/C
12 12 123 12 1212 12 1 23 12
ár fæst æt écga gelacum . # Spræc ða ídes scýl dinga . ‖

1705:

x́ xx x́xx xx # xx xx x́x x́x ‖   3(1)/4   A/F
1 23 123 12 1212 12 12 12 3
ðín ofer þéoda ge hwylce # eal þu hit ge þýldum héal dest |

x́xx x́x x̀ x # xxx x́xx x́ x | 3(1)/3   D/C
123 12 1 2 12123 123 1 2 3
mǽgen mid mód es snỳttrum # ic þe sceal míne gelǽstan |

x́x xx x́x xx # xxx x́x x́ x | 4(1)/3   A/C
12 12 12 12 12123 12 1 2 3
fréoðe swa wit fúr ðum spræcon   # ðu scealt to frófre   wéor þan . |

2995:
x́xx x́ xx x̀x # xxx xx x́x x́x | 3(1)/4   D²/F
123 1 23 12 12123 12 12 12 3
lándes 7 lócenra bèaga   # neðorfte him ða léan oð wítan |

x́x x́ x x̀x ‖   xx xx x́xx x́x ‖   3(1)/4   D²/F
12 1 2 12 12 12 12 123 12 3
món on míddan gèarde ‖ syððа hie ða mǽrða ge slógon . |

4 MEASURING THE RHYTHM OF THE FIVE TYPES

Old English meter is most fully realized in long lines. It is a pattern of two phrase stresses in each of two verses of four members, which are linked together by alliteration. The phrase stresses operate freely in their function of phonological and emphatic prominence; hence they may appear in any position along the verse and long line regardless of the length or brevity of that unit. This freedom of position is one of the classic examples of rhythmical variation in OE meter. A classification of the positions that the phrase stresses most often occupy has been the basis of one of the schools of OE prosody since Sievers first introduced his system of Five Types in 1885, and the classification has also been incorporated into the readings of the school of musical scanners, or equal timers.

Since most of the OE metrical studies have been presented either in relation to or within the framework of the Five Types, it seems necessary to demonstrate the theory of measurement I have presented in chapter iii above in relation to the Five Type system also. There is no problem in doing so, certainly, since measurement should finally reveal this rhythmical variation as well as others more clearly than might be otherwise possible. And any problem that arises in the use of the Five Types is a result of emphasis: too determined an effort to fit every verse into one of five categories puts too much emphasis on one kind of rhythmical variation—the position of the phrase stresses—and too little on the abstract meter and its potential for variation; and an exclusive concentration on verse patterns is also finally misleading since the linking into long lines is an important characteristic of this meter in OE practice.

Measuring a significant number of verses in terms of the Five Types and their subtypes will provide an opportunity to relate my theory not only to Sievers but more specifically to Bliss and to Cable, who have done the most thorough jobs of classifying the rhythmical variations within the Five Types, and also to Pope, whose catalogue of readings of all the verses in *Beowulf* is organized according to the Five Types. Since the works of Pope and Bliss are the most comprehensive and probably the most popular systems now in use, and Cable's is the most recent comprehensive re-alignment of Bliss to Sievers, I will make frequent references to them and demonstrate my system of measurement in irregular timing as it relates to their readings.

As developed in chapter 3, a verse has four members, each of which may be either a syllable or a measure, and we will indicate this difference by spacing between members only in our abstract model. The Five Types are patterns of the phrase-stress occurrences within a verse. According to the theory of five patterns, the two phrase stresses may be distributed in a pattern of alternation from the beginning of the verse: x́ x x́ x (A: which is theoretically extensible to x́xx xxx x́xx xxx, but which I have not found in *Beowulf* longer than x́xx xxx x́x x|); of alternation from the end of the verse: x x́ x x́ (B: extensible to xxx x́xx xxx x́xx, but not found longer than xxx x́xx xx x́x|); or separated as widely as possible with intermediate stress on the second member: x́ x̀ x x́ (E: extensible to x́xx x̀xx xxx x́xx, but more commonly found in x́xx x̀xx xx x́|); or bunched at the beginning with intermediate stress on either the third or fourth member: x́ x́ x̀ x or x́ x́ x x̀ (D: extensible to such a pattern as x́xx x́xx x̀xx xxx, but found extended only to x́x x́xx x̀x x|); or bunched in the middle: (C: extensible to xxx x́xx x́xx xxx, but found closer to xxx x́x x́x x|). That the stresses might not also be bunched toward the end, x x x́ x́ (extensible to a theoretical xxx xxx x́xx x́xx, but found in *Beowulf* as xxx xxx x́xx x́x|), I find difficult to accept, since we find a substantial number of just such patterns in verses usually typed B, C, and A3. We will deal with these as we meet them in the separate types in order to hypothesize a sixth type—F. And if one accepts my hypothesis that a member may be expanded into a measure in any of the four positions, then one must accept the possibility of a final unstressed syllable forming a measure with the final phrase stress in types B and E, although OE practice may have restricted its use.

TYPE A: x́ x x́ x (x́xx xxx x́x x|)

The most common rhythmic pattern in *Beowulf* is type A. In its typical form it is composed of two measures. Rhythmical variations may be noted objectively in the presence of additional syllables and of stress to give such patterns as the following, a by no means exhaustive list:

x́ x x́ x | 16a: lánge   hwíle |
1 2 1 2 3

x́ xx x́ x |					14a: fólce	tofrófre	|
1 23 1 2 3

x́ x x́ x |					82a: héah	7hórn	gèap	|
1 2 1 2 3

x́ x x́ x |					2293b: hórd	wèard	sóhte	|
1 2 1 2 3

x́ xx x́ x |					193a: nýd wràcu	níþ grìm	|
1 23 1 2 3

The last example is closest to incorporating the next type of variation, additional measures. One extra syllable produces a three measure verse, as in the following:

x́x xx x́ x |					2980a: brécan	ofer	bórd	wèal	|
12 12 1 2 3

But the three measures may be as varied as follows:

x́xx xx x́ x |					2690a: ræsde	onðone rófan	|
123 12 1 2 3

x́x xx x́ x |					438a: géolo	rànd	to gúþe	|
12 12 1 2 3

x́ x x́x x |					330a: æsc	hòlt	úfan græg	|
1 2 12 1 2

The last example given (330a) perhaps opens the way to the measurement of some other type A verses; these have two syllables following the second stress and before a |, which must be included as part of this verse since the following verse begins immediately with a primary stress. Such a verse is 621a, with which for purposes of analysis I include the b-verse:

x́x xx x́x x |		dúgu þe	7géo go þe	|	dæl + æghwylcne	|
12 12 12 1 2

Twice in chapter 3 above I discussed a situation of this type. To say it differently here: Several factors support the decision to begin a new measure with the third syllable of *geogope* before the |. Simple grouping in twos and threes requires another word stress among the five pulses from

géo- to *dǽl* and it must fall on the most likely one. Other things being
equal, that would not be immediately before or after a major stress, since
that position is always reduced in stress by such juxtaposition unless at
least secondary stress inheres in the syllable itself. The natural law of
alternation would give more prominence to the syllable following such a
reduced one. In lines like the one we are examining both syllables have
weak stress inherently, although the old dictionary rule for Modern
English would give the third syllable in this case a potential "secondary
accent." Pope too gives a degree of stress to the final syllable:

> dŭguþè ond gĕogoþè   (pp. 253–54)

This is how he reads all lines of this type—he has none stressed in a
pattern of x̆ x̀ x̆ x̀ x. Pope's reading, then, while supporting mine,
implies more of a rhythmical stress distinction between the last two
syllables than I imply with an ictus.[1]

Finally, spacing within words in the manuscript seems to tell us something in this line having three instances of the same metrical variation—in
dugupe and *æghwylcne* as well as in *geogope*. However, any theory interpreting the manuscript spacings is fraught with exceptions and must be
applied very judiciously and in support of other factors which by themselves may explain the situation. Nevertheless, the full space in *dugu pe*
and the admittedly less space but still clear separation in *geo go pe* and
æghwylc ne may tell us that the scribe heard here the undulating influence
of the ictuses which made the syllabic entities more pronounced though
they did not in these cases exhibit intensity.

Verses of this type, including measures which begin on the third weak
syllable of a word followed by |, are not numerous among the type A
verses. In the vast majority of cases (indeed it is difficult to find a good
example) other circumstances exist to allow the syllable to take the third
count. This happens either when the line break is # or when the following
verse begins with unstressed syllables (B and C types and the so-called
anacrustic verses), which allow or cause the line break (|) to become the
first count of a measure in the following verse, as in 52a: (As the reader
may notice, I do not include the line-break symbol in the abstract pattern
provided on the left when it is part of the measurement of the following
verse rather than of the one under consideration.)

x́x xx x́x x
12 12 12 3
52a: hǽleð   under   héofenum | hwa   þæm   hlǽste   on féng #

And there is clearly no problem when the third syllable after the second phrase stress clearly bears secondary stress, as in 688a:

x́x xxx x́x x | hýlde hine þa héaþo dèor | hléor
12 123 12 1 2

Another variation of the A type which is significant rhythmically but measures no differently is that which has an alliterating phrase stress only in the second position. These are Sievers' type A3, for which Bliss uses the symbol a but which Cable restores to A (*MM* 20–30). In my examples below I include again the alliterating word from the second verse in order to point up the pattern.

x́ x x́ x | 391a: eów het sécgan | síge
1 2 1 2 3

x́ xx x́ x | 53a: Dá wæs on búrgum | béowulf
1 23 1 2 3

x́xx xxx x́ x   1671a: íc hit þe þonne ge háte | þæt þu on héo-
123 123 1 2

These are light verses rhythmically, and this lightness may be compensated for, as in the last two examples, by additional unstressed syllables.

The type A verse which has two alliterating stresses but has in addition one or more unstressed syllables preceding the first of these (so-called anacrusis) shows significant variation only because it has to be labelled type A in a Five Type system. Its unstressed beginning gives the composite rhythm an initial thetic (upbeat) movement. As with B and C types, the preceding line break may take the ictus for this first measure, or, the initial unstressed syllable may be the third count of the measure that began with the final syllable of the preceding verse, as in the following:

| x x́ x x́x | 2629a: ´ | gewác æt wíge #
2 3 1 2 12 3

Or, when there are two or three preliminary unstressed syllables, they may simply form a measure by themselves:

xx x́ xx x́x | 1248a: ge æt hám ge on hérge |
12 1 23 12 3

This last is something different. When grouped into member-measures, the pattern is much closer to B than to A. I wonder if a full measure before the first phrase stress can really be called an anacrusis. The final un-stressed syllable seems more naturally part of the final, phrase-stressed member of a B pattern, than do the first two syllables seem anacrustic.

The pattern in the following verse favors a B reading even more clearly:

xx x́x xx x́x   1711a: # Ne ge wéox   he him   to will an |
12 12 12 12

All of the type A verses with disyllabic anacrusis, as given by Pope, follow this pattern, except the following one, which seems closer to the extended C types:

xx x́x x́x x̀ | 1563a: hege féng   þa fétel   hilt |
12 12 12 1 2

although the secondary stress on the final syllable would render it suspect as a C type to most OE prosodists. Perhaps some of the verses with monosyllabic anacrusis bear more kinship to type C also. However, such a hypothesis would demand an individual treatment of the verses which I cannot give them here. My purpose is to suggest the limitations of the Five Types as a metrical system by showing what simple measurement reveals in the different situations, rather than to present a new reading of all verses of suspect types.

TYPE B: x x́ x x́ (xxx x́x xx x́x)

Type B verses are always composed of at least three measures, since although they are usually rhythmically lighter than other types (A, D, E), they include within their measures one or both of the line breaks sur-rounding them. This rule is absolute regarding the one at the end of the verse. It always provides the second count to complete the measure begun by the second phrase stress. In addition, the preceding | line break is always involved when there is only one unstressed syllable at the begin-ning of the verse, and often when there are two:

| x x́ x x́ #   61b: | 7hálga tíl #
1 2 1 2 1 23

| xx x́ x x́ | 615a: | 7þa   fréolic wíf |
1 23 1 2 1 2

However, the reading of verses beginning with two unstressed syllables depends entirely on the syntax, since two syllables can easily become a complete measure. When three unstressed syllables precede the first stress, they usually begin with the ictus, as in the following:

xxx x́ x x́ #   108b: þæs þe he ábel slóg #
123 1 2 1 23

However, the natural speech rhythm may instead make of them two measures, employing again the preceding line break, as in the following where my abstract pattern makes the first syllable a species of anacrusis:

| x xx x́ x x́ | 300a: | þæt þone hílde ráes |²
1 2 12 1 2 1 2

When additional unstressed syllables are introduced at the beginning of the verse, on the other hand, they may fill two measures without involving the preceding line break at all:

xx xx x́x x́ | 1809b: sǽgde him þæs léanes þánc |
12 12 12 1 2

Or again they may involve the preceding boundary in the first of these, depending on the natural speech rhythm, since any measure may be either a binary or a ternary group. In all of these it is a matter of the material before the first stress being extended. But such an extension makes the pattern of the original four simple beats in 1809b into x x x́ x́, and the same occurs in many other B type verses. We will speak of them again later.

When additional syllables are introduced between the two phrase stresses we remain closer to the simple typical pattern, and a number of variations are possible. Ordinarily, the extra syllable is gathered up in the measure of the first phrase stress:

x x́ xx x́ | 80a: # He béot ne aléh |
123 1 23 1 2

xx x́x x x́ #   756a: secan déofla ge drǽg #
12 12 3 123

When the measures are thus expanded, however, another rhythmic factor may come into sufficient prominence to affect the verse metrically. This is the caesura within the verse. In most of the cases we have covered thus far,

I accept Bliss's placement of the caesura as operating rhythmically as a word or phrase boundary with relative value up to, but not including, a full pulse. I maintain this conservative view even for the majority of these verses of type B in which Bliss makes much of a distinction between the 3B2, for example, and the 3B* (between xx-xx|- and xx-x|x-). However, in such verses as the following, the caesura as a phrase boundary may well come into such prominence as to take a full pulse, thus providing another measure:

#x x́+ xx x́ | 272b: # þuwást + gif   hit   ís |
123 12 12 1 2

And when there are three unstressed syllables between the two phrase stresses, I suggest that using the caesura as the metrical ictus initiating the additional measure may well provide the best interpretation for performance:

xx x́xx +x x́ | 2997a: 7ða   íofore + for géaf |
12 123 12 1 2

However, Pope reads this verse, and others like it, with the equivalent of an ictus on the third syllable of *Iofore:*

ondða Io-fo-re for geaf   (p. 284)

I can accept this, especially since it is so close to the readings we made above of type A verses requiring a metrical ictus on a third syllable with weak stress before the line break.

TYPE C: x x́ x́ x (xxx x́x x́x xx)

Type C verses are characterized in their simplest form by a word boundary (+) requiring a full pulse between the two phrase stresses, in the position where Sievers, Bliss, and Joynes all agree that there is a caesura. As a consequence of this pulse, verses of this type regularly contain three measures since a light measure always precedes the first phrase stress, initiated either by the previous line break or by the first of several unstressed syllables. As in type B verses, this preliminary measure (or measures) will depend on both the number and the character of these syllables. Thus we have such simple typical patterns as these:

| x x́+ x́ x | 4a: | Oft scýld + scéfing |
1 2 12 1 2 3

| x x́+ x́ x | 253b: | on lánd + déna |
1 2 12 1 2 3

xx x́+ x́ x | 187a: æfter déað + dǽge |
12 12 1 2 3

The word boundary pulse, however, may be replaced by a second syllable without destroying the character of the C type, as in the following:

| x x́x x́ x | 106b: | for scrífen hǽfde
1 2 12 1 2 3

xx x́x x́ x | 188a: 7tofǽder fǽþmum |
12 12 1 2 3

´ | x x́x x́ x | 604a: ´ | to mé do módig |
1 2 3 12 1 2 3

The close similarity of these last verses to the type A with anacrusis cannot be overlooked. That kinship is brought out, of course, by the vocalization of the pulse between the two phrase stresses with a distinct sound shape or syllable, as opposed to a boundary sound.

In a very few cases the second phrase stress of a type C is followed by two unstressed syllables, creating the same situation we experienced in the type A verses with three counts before the |. Such a verse is 164a, with which I include the alliterating stress of the following verse to show the pattern:

#x x́x x́x x | 164a: # swa féla fýrene | féond
123 12 12 1 2

Such verses present no problems and are clearly type C.

Verses which seem to me less legitimately C types are those that have two preliminary measures of unstressed syllables and only a very light final syllable. These are the ones, like those found among the Bs also, whose primary stresses are bunched at the end of the verse (x x x́ x́), as in the following:

xx xx x́+ x́x   441b: seþe hine déað + nímeð (#)
12 12 12 12

When found in this extended form, the issue is too cloudy, perhaps, to arouse concern. But when this form is clearly evident in a manuscript verse of four simple beats, as the following:

```
| x x x́+ x́ #          1116b: | 7on bæl + dón #
  1 2 3 12  1 23
```

editors have always required the archaic pronunciation of two syllables, even though the tenth-century scribe wrote the monosyllable he must have heard in the recitation. Verses of this kind fit within the rhythmical potential of the OE meter with no difficulty. Whether they were part of the early practice in that meter is a question I cannot answer without much further study. However, the pattern as realized in extended verses that we have discussed may have caused it to appear in the four-syllable verse by the tenth century without offending the ears. In any case, I prefer to measure these verses as I did in 1116b above, and as follows, simply allowing the line-break pulse to complete the measure which centuries earlier was filled by a syllable pulse:

```
x xx x́+ x́ #            1058b: swa he   nu gít + déð #
1 23 12  1 23
```

However, an archaic pronunciation of two syllables, or of a glide, is certainly acceptable also. OE meter provides for just this kind of flexibility. Boundary pulses could always fill up measures, and as the language changed they simply did so more often. In linguistic history this is the natural rhythmic compensation that operates when such syllables as inflected endings, for example, are dropped under the influence of stress, when a language becomes heavily monosyllabic, and when proclitics are used minimally, as in contemporary poetry. Hence, I do not object to these words (*don, deð, teon*, etc.) being "de-contracted" for the sake of our recognizing their original shapes. I am suggesting only that the scribe in the tenth century would have found nothing amiss rhythmically in hearing them as one syllable.

Nor do I propose, as long as the words are clearly "de-contractable," to take these verses whose basic pattern seems to be x x x́ x́ rather than x x́ x́ x out of the C classification. On the other hand, a recognition of the legitimacy of the pattern (x x x́ x́) would perhaps remove some of the difficulties for prosodists who still work within the Five Type framework.

Many of the verses classified by Sievers and by Pope as C types had been reclassified by Bliss as d1, d2, and d3, and some of the Bs had been reclassified as d4 and d5. I accept Cable's rereading of all of these lines as normal on the grounds that the rhythm of poetic phrasing will give syntactic and semantic prominence to a second position in a verse. Therefore, I omit here my own arrival at the same conclusion by using the less tangible evidence from manuscript spacing and rhythmic measurement.

TYPE D: x́ x́ x x (x̌x x́x xx xx)

Type D is rhythmically heavier than the other types, not because it usually has more measures (we saw in B and C that additional measures seem to add no rhythmical weight), but because both of its phrase stresses occur at the beginning of the verse and usually rest on a heavy monosyllable followed by a compound carrying a secondary as well as a primary stress, or followed by more than one word which may then be given additional stress according to interpretation. Besides, such juxtaposition of stresses always forces one, and often two, of the members to be extended by a boundary pulse into a measure, even when the verse contains only four syllables as in the following typical examples: (Since the arrangement of the D type in its shortest form usually creates before the end of the verse a situation of three syllables of which two are relatively heavy, in my examples I will always include the first word of the following verse in order to show the consequent treatment of the three.)

x́+ x́+ x̌ x | 31a: léof + lánd + frùma | lánge
12 12 1 2 3

x́+ x́ x̌ x ‖   57a: héah + héalf dène ‖ héold
12 1 2 3 12

What is illustrated here is perhaps more obvious visually than orally and is another variation of what was discussed on pp. 60–61 above. Here a metrically significant secondary stress is involved. It may be handled in either of the ways illustrated in 31a and 57a above. There is an audible rhythmical difference between them in view of which my conservative attitude toward overstressing has always prompted me to favor the second reading when possible. However, the first example with its free use of word-boundary pulses is not at all foreign to our ears now used to contemporary poetry, and, just as it did for the poet, the rhythmical adjustment occurs without conscious effort on the part of any reader or reciter who has a sense of rhythm. Perhaps there is something of a law of compensation operating here. Rhythmic movements will complete themselves. If the first example (31a) is read without an ictus on *fruma,* the reader will automatically lengthen the line break to form its own measure before attacking the next primary stress. We can signify this additional length by adding a second bar (‖), as in the following:

x́+ x́ x̀ x ‖   54a: léof + léod   cẏning ‖ lónge
12 1 2 3 12

By the same principle, in the second example, if the reader makes *healf* a measure in itself with a word-boundary pulse and starts a new measure with *dene,* he will probably shorten the following line break to include it in the one measure with *dene,* although most editors use a semicolon. Hence, in cases such as these a reader may legitimately choose either of the following alternate readings, depending on his preference for over-stressing:

x́+ x́ x̀ x | 376a: héard + hér cùmen | sohte
12 1 2 3 1

x́+ x́+ x̀ x | héard + hér +cùmen | sohte
12 12 1 2 3

The word-boundary pulses in verses of type D are easily replaced by syllables, as in the following:

x́x x́ x̀ x | 21a: frómum féoh   gìf tum | on
12 1 2 3 1

x́+ x́x x̀ x | 1847a: híld + héoru   grìm   me | hréþ
12 12 1 2 3

An important variation in the rhythm of the D types is found when the intermediate stress is delayed until the last syllable of the verse (x́ x́ x x̀: Sievers' type D4, and Bliss's D4, 5, and 6). Cable finds these different enough to call them an additional type between D and E (see *MM* 70–82). Actually, this variation makes the measurement easier since the secondary stress in such an environment will always take an ictus, and there is eliminated some of the seeming force in having two of the verse's members lengthened by word-boundary pulses. Thus we have:

x́+ x́ x x̀ | 1307a: hár +hílde   rìnc | on
12 1 2 1 2

or expanded with additional syllables:

x́+ x́ xx x̀x | 1747a: wǫ́m + wún   dor   be bǫ̀dum | wér-
12 1 23 12 3

x̀x x́ x x̀ | 1359a: frécne   fén ge làd | ðær
12 1 2 1 2

But the majority of type D verses, according to Bliss's statistics, have
only tertiary or weak stress where the above have secondary. Cable,
following his analysis of the same conditions in type E, would regard them
as intermediate metrical stress regardless of their linguistic stress, and I
agree with his argument. However, such verses may call for a rhythmical
adjustment that affects the measurement, and an adjustment that may
reflect any one of the above readings but may also cause those verses
requiring an additional ictus before the (|) line break to take it on the last
syllable. It can do so, not because it is stronger than the preceding
syllable—which it is not—but because it is stronger than the (|) line break
that follows it:

x́+ x́ x x | 176a: wíg + wéor þunga | wǫ́rdum
12 1 2 1 2

On the other hand, the reader can again give the line break the two
counts of a measure, thus allowing the three-syllable word to read as
x x x ‖. Cable's melodic nuance (see my p. 65 above) is the best
1 2 3
illustration of how the speech apparatus can provide sufficient prominence
to the intermediate stress without its taking the ictus.

Although my discussion of the metrical reading represented in these
verses was largely given in the section on type A, I nevertheless consider
type D to provide something of a prototype for the readings in the two
patterns: x́ x́ x̀ x and x́ x́ x x̀ because intermediate stress is part of its
pattern. This is only to call attention again to the kinship existing between
the various types, for so often their edges seem to flow into each other.
And again in my reading of this subtype, I tend to follow intuitively the
manuscript spacing to a rather significant degree. However, as I said
above, a theory of manuscript spacing is fraught with exceptions—as in
3178–82 where the scribe was crowding in order to avoid using another
sheet of parchment. It can also be dangerous. For example, a theory that
says "syllables capable of bearing primary metrical stress shall be so
written that their stress function is clearly indicated,"[3] would probably
take line 2312b; sœcyninga, out of type D where it clearly belongs.

TYPE E: x́ x̀ x x́ (x́x x̀x xx x́x)

Type E can be a much lighter verse than type D, in spite of the fact that verses are sometimes given alternate D and E readings. The lightness may be due to the fact that its two phrase stresses are so widely separated, and also to the fact that in its typical form of four syllables it has only one fully-sounded measure and a second one completed by the line break.

x́ x̀ x x́ #   190a: síngàla séað #
1 2 3 1 23

x́ x̀ x x́ #   78a: héal æ̀rna mǽst #
1 2 3 1 23

x́ x̀ x x́ | 783b: nórð dènum stód |
1 2 3 1 2

I find it rhythmically preferable to measure these verses in this way, although there are cases where it might be preferable to give the first phrase stress a word-boundary pulse, thus giving the secondary stress a new ictus. Such a case might be the following:

x́+ x̀ x x́ | 8b: wéorð + mỳndum þáh |
12 1 2 1 2

And this count is no different from that of all the verses which have an unstressed syllable with the first phrase stress, as the following:

x́x x̀ x x́ | 93a: wlíte bèorhtne wáng | swa wǽt er
12 1 2 1 2

    When extra syllables occur after the secondary stress, however, one of several alternative measurements may be employed, depending on the syntax. For example, there is no problem when the secondary stress already takes the ictus:

x́x x̀ xx x́ | 658a: háfa nù 7ge héald |
12 1 23 1 2

But when the secondary stress would not ordinarily take the ictus, it may do so in order to allow for the extra syllable:

x́+ x̀x x x́ #   1241b: flét + ræ̀ste ge béag #
12 12 3 1 23

However, in such a case the caesura may assert itself, as it does in some of the B type verses, thus obviating the necessity for heightening the secondary stress to that extent. This would give the following reading:

x̋ x̀x +x x̋ #   flét   ræste + ge   béag #
1 23 12 1 23

This reading is even more desirable in those cases where the first syllables were originally compounds, as in:

x̋ x̀x +x x̋ #   455a: wélàndes + ge wéorc #
1 23 12 1 23

However, in that verse as in the following it is equally valid to begin the extra little measure on the third syllable:

x̋x x̀x xx x̋ | 911a: fǽder æ̀þelum   on fón |
12 12 12 1 2

   There may be a still different measurement if more of the words are monosyllables. For example:

x̋ x̀ xx x̋ #   2489b: féorh swèng   neof téah #
1 2 12 1 23

x̋ x̀x xx x̋ | 2691b: héals èalne   ymbe féng |
1 23 12 1 2

However, both of these verses may be read as well with an ictus on the secondary stress. Such an interpretation makes for a quite different rhythm, one that, in the first example, is much closer to that of type D.

x̋+ x̀ xx x̋ #   2489b: féorh + swèng   neof téah #
12 1 23 1 23

In the second of the two examples, the rhythmic effect would be more undulating because of the number of measures, since the extra syllable with the secondary stress requires that *ymbe* still constitute a measure:[4]

x̋+ x̀x xx x̋ | 2691b: héals + èalne   ymbe féng |
12 12 12 1 2

   Just as there are heavier verses of the E type, so there may be very light ones, related perhaps to the normal E as A3 or Bliss's a is to the normal A, and his d to type C. The following is certainly such a verse:

```
x́x x̀ x x́ |            3027a: þénden  hèwið  wúlf |
12 1 2 1 2                        '       '      '
```

However, the other six examples of Bliss's type e, it seems to me, are more accurately read according to Sievers' (and Pope's) classifications of A and B, as Cable reads them. Light in a somewhat different way are such verses as these:

```
x́ x x x́ #           · 2150a: líssa   gelóng #
1 2 3 1 23                    '       '

x́ x x x́ |             747b: rǽhte   on géan |
1 2 3 1 2                    '        '
```

Bliss classifies them as 2E1a whereas Pope puts them in his type F, as he does also with 3027b. Cable considers these two verses unmetrical because of the absence of any possibility of secondary stress (*MM*, 63). There is no difficulty in measuring the verses, but measurement does not reveal the basis on which Cable judges them unmetrical.

Another light rhythmical variation but still an authentic E pattern is present in two lines which Bliss indexes as remnants and Pope classifies this time as E:

```
x́ x xx x́ |           183b: wá bið  þǽm  ðe  scéal |
1 2 12 1 2                   '      '        '

x́ x x̀x x́ |           186b: wél  bið  þǽm  þe mót |
1 2 12 1 2                   '      '       '
```

A PROPOSED TYPE F: x x x́ x́ (xxx xx x́x x́x)

I began my study for the purpose of measuring the verses of *Beowulf* simply as lengths of linguistic and rhythmic material in order to demonstrate that such material in poetry can be measured into unequal measures. I did not start out by measuring the material in the Five Types of Sievers, nor in the four members of Kaluza (Cable's work did not appear until after I had measured every line in the manuscript and had my typescript in the hands of a publisher). Nor did I allow myself to think in such terms as anacrusis, resolution, and long vowels. Perhaps it was this release from previous restrictions that allows my measurement process to reveal what I consider a few insights.

The first of these is the suggestion that four-member verses typically filled with four syllables can be extended from two- to three- to four-measure verses theoretically containing twelve syllables. Another (following from the first) is the proposal that if the two phrase stresses of the meter can be found on any of the four members, then there are six possible patterns rather than five. This suggestion is derived from identifying the four members in four-measure verses where the sixth pattern is clearly attested.

Cable concludes (*MM* 92) that "four metrical units necessarily produce five patterns—not more than five, and no fewer." I find the argument leading up to his conclusion unconvincing, although I recognize that the five patterns "emerge from conditions that [he] would impose, for independent reasons, upon the meter" (*MM* 88). One of these conditions is not stated but implied in the "contour" patterns he devises: A: $1\diagdown2\diagup3\diagdown4$; B: $1\diagup2\diagdown3\diagup4$; C: $1\diagup2\diagdown3\diagdown4$; D1: $1\diagdown2\diagdown3\diagdown4$; D2,E: $1\diagdown2\diagdown3\diagup4$. That condition is that the fourth position is always the stress "contour" of the ending position of the preceding diagonal line. This is not true of any of the preceding positions. Their prominence is indicated by the beginning position of the following diagonal. Hence, by not using a diagonal line after the fourth number, it is not possible to describe a pattern of ˜ ˘ ´ ´, even though it is possible to have the two clashing stresses within the line.[5]

Furthermore, in revising the old method of "positing five completely different kinds of feet" (´x; x´; ´; ´´x; ´x`) which "occur arbitrarily in eight combinations" to read that "a verse has four metrical positions that may occur in any combination, with the condition that the second of two clashing stresses cannot be heavier," he nevertheless seems to be retaining in his combinations the concept of feet. (There is no "foot" like xx´; a "foot" of ´ cannot follow another "foot.") Otherwise, the four positions will form the six patterns I find in *Beowulf*. The alternative fault in his statement would be an implication that when the positions pattern as ˘ ˜ ´ ´ the second stress would be heavier than the first. But this would contradict all the evidence he provided in his book to show that "the first of two consecutive stresses must always be the heavier" (*MM* 73). And it would not be borne out by the verses where the sixth pattern is evident.

I called attention to many of these verses when discussing hypermetric lines and types B and C above. Here it might be more illuminating to take those patterns that John Pope catalogues which reduce to the abstract x x x́ x́ in his readings. The first of these belong to his first half-line—type B: 7, 21, 26, 29, and 48. One of each appears below, first in Pope's notation, and then with my measuring applied. In noting an analogy between our two ways of counting time, it must be remembered that in 4/8 time a quarter note denotes two pulses (beats) which constitute one of my little measures.

7. |♪♪♪♪ |♪♪♩ | 2619: þeah ðe he his bróðer béarn |
xx xx   xx x́ |
12 12   12 1 2

21. |♪♪♪♪ |♫♫♩ | 182: ne hie huru héo fena hélm |
xx xx   x́xx x́ |
12 12   123 1 2

26. |♪♪♪♪ |♪♪♪♪| 718: nǽfre   he on áldor dágum |
xx xx   xx x́x |
12 12   12 12 3

29. |♪♪♪♪ |♩♪♪♪| 2636: þæt þe him ða gúð ge táwa |
xx xx   xx x́x |
12 12   12 12 3

48. ♪| ♪ ♪ ♪ ♪|♪ ♫♪♪| 1484: mæg þonne on þǽm gólde ongítan |
xxx xx   x́xx x́x |
123 12   123 12 3

Pope's 7, 21, and 26 are found in b-verses also, and 8 in the b-verse is close enough to 7 above that it need not be repeated. Other examples found in b-verses but not in a-verses are the following:

14. |♪♪♪♪ |♩ ♪♪ | 2280: oððæt hyne án+abéalch |
xx xx   x́+x x́ |
12 12   1 23 1 2

37. |♪♪♪♪ |♪♫♩ | 968: no ic him þæs géorne æt féalh |
xx xx   x́xx x́ |
12 12   123 1 2

38. |♪♪♫ |♪♫♩ | 626: þæs ðe hire se wílla ge lámp |
xx xxx   x́xx x́ |
12 123   123 1 2

39. |♫♪♪ |♪♫♩ | 970: hwæþere he his fólme for lét |
xxx xx   x́xx x́ |
123 12   123 1 2

40. ♪| ♪ ♪♪♪|♪♫♩ | 1585: toðæs ·þe he   onrǽste ge séah |
   |x x+x xx   x́xx x́ |
    2 123 12   123 1 2

The manuscript punctum in the final example is one of the thirteen found within verses. It seems to me to indicate something like a word boundary for lengthening, which may be best interpreted with an ictus on *þæs* and with the optional extra pulse, giving the verse four measures and an additional anacrusis. Or the punctum could indicate a nuance that put the ictus on *þe:* xx + xxx x́xx x́ |

                    '   '   '

Pope's type C, showing a phrase stress pattern of x x x́ x́, is in the categories of a-verses that follow:

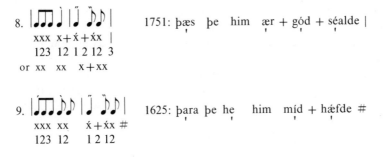

7. |♪♪♪♪ |♩♪♪ | 1051: þara þe mid   béoẃúlfe |
   xx xx   x́+x́xx |
   12 12   1 2 12 3

16. |♪♪♪♪ |♪♪ ♪♪| 677: no ic me   an hére wǽsmun |
   xx xx   x́x   x́x |
   12 12   12   12 3

29. |♪♪♪♪ |♩ ♪♪| 1342: seþe æfter sínc + gýfan |
   xx xx   x́+x́x |
   12 12   12 12 3

31: ♪| ♪♪♪♪ |♩ ♪♪| 2528: þæt ic wið þone   gúð + flógan |
   | x xx xx   x́+x́x |
   2 3 12 12   12 12 3

And in b-verses, in addition to the same categories of 7, 16, 29, and 31 above, it is found also in the following:

8. |♫♩ |♩ ♪♪| 1751: þæs þe him ær + gód + séalde |
   xxx x+x́+x́xx |
   123 12 1 2 12 3
  or xx   xx   x+xx

9. |♫♪♪ |♩ ♪♪| 1625: þara þe he   him míd + hǽfde #
   xxx xx   x́+x́x #
   123 12   1 2 12

30. | ♪♪♪ ♪♪| ♩ ♪♪| 1485: | þonne he on þæt sínc + stárað
| xx xxx   x́ + x́x
1 23 123   1 2 12

The last example given was used in chapter 3 (p. 104) as part of an eight-measure long line. As can be noted in my abstract pattern (beneath Pope's), every one of the verses counts into four measures; hence each will be found in a long line of at least six, seven, or eight measures. In all of these categories Pope included a total of seventy-six verses. If we add the eight that I patterned as type F among the hypermetric lines on pp. 73–74 and those verses which in the tenth century contained contracted verbs, we begin to get upward of a hundred verses showing the pattern of my proposed type F. Since the majority are clearly verses with extended material, it may be that the pattern x x x́ x́ in OE practice could only surface in such long verses. But when it does surface, it can only lead to certain conclusions, if we are to maintain both the assumption that verses always have four and only four members and my further assumption that a member could be extended to a measure but in *Beowulf* never beyond that.

The first conclusion is that when four syllables (or two measures) precede the first phrase stress, the first phrase stress is thereby preceded by *two* of the four members. This cannot happen in the B or C type patterns. And rhythmically speaking, for example in verse 1051a given above, there is no likeness of movement between the theses (upbeats) of *para pe mid* and the final *-e* of *beowulfe,* which is patterned into a type C. Likewise, in verse 2619a, there is not the alternating thesis-arsis-thesis-arsis of a type B pattern.

A second conclusion is that if the four members of the abstract pattern can generate additional syllables (and whole measures), then an unstressed syllable can theoretically follow in a final phrase-stressed position, as it does in a number of the examples from Pope's categories of type B. OE practice, of course, may have restricted its doing so or may have required that when such an additional syllable appeared, resolution had to be possible. I have no difficulty in admitting such restrictions in the practice of a meter that has a long tradition, especially an oral one. But we must accept those verses in which the poet bends the restrictions.

Perhaps in the OE traditional practice there was also a restriction against a rhythmical pattern of my type F: x x x́ x́, which restriction the poet was able to "bend" only in extended verses. After having heard the pattern often enough, the ear would eventually find it acceptable in verses of four syllables (which are closest to the abstract meter) when phonological development changed the form of words, as we see in the contracted verbs.

I cannot draw any further conclusion about the OE practice in regard either to the assumptions (1) that a verse has only four members, (2) that a member can generate one measure but no more, and (3) that two phrase stresses will occur in a verse on any two of the four members, thus forming any one of six possible patterns, or to my suggested conclusion that since these assumptions are fulfilled in the verses of *Beowulf* they are characteristic of all OE poetry. Further conclusions would require the same kind of measurement applied to the rest of the poetic corpus, especially to those "hypermetric" lines of the other poems indexed by Bliss (pp. 162–168). But I do suggest further that the admission of type F (not to be confused with Pope's F for "unclassified remainders") would remove some of the ambiguity within the present Five Type system.

5 THE SUSPECT VERSES
AND A SUMMARY

*T*he tenth century manuscript of the *Beowulf* may not have preserved the original poem either in its ancient oral form or in its probable composition during the early Christian centuries of Anglo-Saxon England. But it has kept for us this greatest of surviving English epic-elegies in a form that the scops and their listeners surely heard as acceptable in their native tradition. And the native tradition had not died. Both *The Battle of Brunanburg* and *The Battle of Maldon* testify to a tenth-century knowledge and practice of its ancient and typical form. Perhaps, then, not all of the lines in the *Beowulf* that have always been emended for metrical reasons are actually unmetrical. This is not to say that the *Beowulf* scribe made no errors. We know that he did because he or a proofreader made corrections in a number of places; but where a correction was not made there is less probability of an error existing.

From among the emendations made historically for metrical reasons the three-syllable verses are perhaps the easiest to accommodate into the meter, and some are now being retained in the textual editions.[1] They are still being dealt with separately in metrical analyses because they do not conform to Sievers' Five Types. Pope finds it least difficult to accommodate them since his theory is one of timing. He creates his own type F for such verses as these since, as we have suggested, the system of Five types is probably too limited for OE meter.

However, three instances of three syllables standing alone for a verse in the manuscript probably were errors. One is *hafelan* in line 1372 where the scribe or his proofreader inserted a colon (:) surely to call attention to an omission. A colon was used also at the end of lines 2488 and 3136, although in these cases there is sufficient space around the colons to suggest that they were inscribed along with the text, and the b-verses they follow are not deficient in any way. 3136a is a three-syllable verse (*har   hilde*) which is little different metrically from 947a *secg   betsta* (which is never emended); however, the a-verse in line 2488 is the single instance of a two-syllable verse: *hreas   blac,* and since the use of the colon is so similar to that in 1372, I can accept the same interpretation for the colons in these two instances and assume that the scribe was noting an omission. I do so with some reservations since I have no problem reading the verses as metrically harmonious with the others around them.

The free play of threes and twos in the number of measures in verses and long lines makes for interesting speculation in regard to those which are always emended. As we demonstrated above, measuring the long lines reveals that they may range from four to eight measures. In other words, some long lines are twice as long as others, and rhythmically they feel twice as long. For example, 109 could be heard thus: *Nege   feoh   he | þære   fæhðe | ac he   hine | feor   for wræc |*. There are other long lines, especially those with seven measures, which have a rhythmical likeness to three verses. Line 61 with only six measures is a kind of prototype: *heoro gar · 7hroð gar   7halga   til* (xxx + xxx | xxxx #). And the point in the manuscript line (to which I assign a boundary pulse) dramatizes that the scribe felt this. I suggest that this kind of variation within the OE poetic lines could give natural rise to the perhaps rare but nevertheless permissible use, without rhythmic shock, of a long line which is closer to a verse in substance, and also of a single verse between two long lines. It seems to me that both such possibilities are present in a manuscript reading of *Beowulf*. But where they are found, editors have done one of three things to circumvent our recognizing them: they have added entire verses in three cases and two verses in another; they have added words whenever the material seemed insufficient for the two verses in the long line (or for one of the verses); and in addition, in some dozen verses they have added words to provide the alliterative pattern, which is then invoked to "prove" the rule that OE poetry "always" carried its key alliteration in the first stress position of the second verse.

The first suggestion (that the poet may have given us some long lines that have the rhythmic feel of only one verse) may be the answer for the manuscript reading of

> 3101: Uton   nu   efstan   oðre |

which seems to pattern less awkwardly as two verses

>   x́ x x̀ | x́ x x x́ x |
>   1 2 1 2 1 2 1 2 3

than as a single verse, which is the other alternative if the editors' word [*siðe*] is not added.[2] After the following verse, the editors have added another entire verse to complete a line:

2792: breost   hord   þurh bræc # (x́ x̀ x x́)

I suggest that this verse may be a common ground between the case of two verses having the rhythmic feel of one and that of a single verse intervening between two full lines. With the following two, for example, the editors always add a full verse also (I include the preceding and following verses with them):

Snýredon   æt sómne | þa   sécg   wísode |

403:    un   der   héoro tes   hróf |
       12   3   1 2 3   1 2

héard   under   hélme | þæt he on héoðe   gestód

In 403 there is a natural link through the alliteration to the following verse, another device that would have prevented any rhythmic shock. And in the other:

blíð heort   bódode # þa com béorht   scácan #

1803:   scáþan   on ét ton #
                 1 2   3 1 2 12

wǽron   ǽþelingas | éft   to léodum |

there is an alliterative link to the final word of the preceding verse, as there is also a contrastive link in the thought. If these could be accepted as one-verse lines, as I suggest they might, then some of the cases in which editors have added single words to complete the insufficient material in one of the verses might also revert to one-verse lines. Line 3086 is an example:

grímme ge góngen # wæs þæt gífeðe   to swíð |

3086: þeðone þýder on týhte #
      1 2 3 1 2 3 1 2 12

Íc wæs þær ínne | 7þæt   éall   geond   séh

And line 139 is a somewhat heavier example:

þa   wæs   éað   fýnde | þe him   élles   hwǽr |

139:                    gerúmlicor   rǽste |
                    3 1 2 3   1 2 3

béd   æfter   búrum | ðahim ge béacnod   wǽs |

One of the long lines so emended provokes a different handling, however. I suggest that in lines 1328–29 the verses may be satisfactorily divided in the following way, which avoids any necessity for adding a word after *ærgod* and provides a rhythm that heightens the comparison of the "swylc-swylc" clauses.

    x́ xx x́ xx # x́ x x x́ |
    1 23 1 2312 1 2 3 1 2

1328: e o f e r a s   c n y s e d a n s w y l c   s c o l d e   e o r l

    x́ x x́ x | x x́ xx x́ #
    1 2 1 2 1 2 1 23 123

    w e s a n   æ r g o d s w y l c   æ s c h e r e   w æ s

And if the alliterative pattern becomes an exception, it is no more exceptional than what is found in a number of other unemended cases, as will be seen below. A somewhat different case is that of 389 and 390. The manuscript has material for two verses which make metrical and syntactical sense as they stand, for inflection and sentence-terminal boundaries are sufficient to show the transition in recitation. However, editors have interposed two more verses between these two:

g e s á g a   h i m   e a c   w ó r d u m | þ æ t h i e   s i n t   w í l c ú m a n

d é n i g a   l é o d u m # w ó r d i n n e a b é a d #

As the line stands, however, it has no alliteration, although *word* does alliterate with *wilcuman* in the previous line.

These last examples have moved the discussion out of the realm of measurement and into the question of alliteration. And there are enough lines in *Beowulf* that have been emended or read unnaturally for the purposes of alliteration to demand a word on that subject.

SUSPECT ALLITERATION

Early in chapter iii I stated that the pattern of linking two verses into long lines by means of alliteration on certain of the phrase stresses is one remove from, but nevertheless part of, the meter as practiced in OE poetry. For alliteration does not occur in the same way in every long line; there is a difference between the constant pattern of two phrase stresses in a verse of four members and the fluctuating pattern of three or two or two-plus-two alliterating phonemes linking two verses together. Hence, I suggested that the alliteration is one remove from—an overlay of—a clearly irregular pattern against the "static" pattern of two four-member verses and four phrase stresses.

Alliteration[3] is the phonetic device employed in that kind of meter which patterns phrase stresses in phrasal-line units rather than patterning metrical ictuses in line units of predetermined length. Rhyme is employed in the latter meters where the likeness of final sounds is ideally suited to signalling the end of the like-length units. Alliteration, on the other hand, signals the prominent syllable which is a phrase stress of the pattern, thus reinforcing the synthesis of the rhythmic movements in syntactic and semantic phrases. This reinforcement would result in childish sing-song if it were consistently patterned exactly as two or three or (worst of all) four to a long line; hence, the poetic necessity of irregular patterning, at least in the verses of average length. When longer verses are linked into very long lines, the pattern becomes more consistently three to a long line,[4] and it does so to reinforce the poetic unity of the verses which might otherwise seem like prose.

The function of alliteration, then, is something somewhat different from the function of an abstract pattern which is the basic meter, and in OE practice it was built on—geared to—a principle of irregularity. Perhaps this principle accounts (as much at least as the inference of scribal error) for the fact that at least twenty-two long lines of *Beowulf,* as the scribe recorded them, have no alliteration; and at least six others have none in the b-verse, although they have two in the a-verse (a pattern of a a x x). All have been emended either by the insertion of an alliterating word or by the replacement of a word (often the first element of a compound) with one that gives the long line a pattern of alliteration. Long lines with no alliteration are as clear in syntax and meter as the following (I provide the emendations in brackets below the line and directly under the word replaced, or straddling the space when the word is added.):

965: | þæt he for   hánd + grípe | mínum   scólde |
                          [mu n d]

                             +
461: | mid wílfínga || ða hine   gára   cýn |
                                    [We d e]

949: níwe   síbbe # nebið þe   ǽnigre   gád |
                                  [n]

1981: geond þæt síde réced | hǽreðes   dóhtor |
                  [hǽl]

586: f á g u m   s w é o r   d u m ‖ n o i c   þ ǽ s + g ý l p e ‖
                                    [f e l a]

Long lines with alliteration only in the a-verse have been handled as in the following:

2341: l í n d   w i ð   l í g e # s c e o l d e   þ é n d + d á g a |
                                    [l æ n]

  307: s í g o n æ t   s ó m n e | o þ þ æ t h y   ǽ l + t í m b r e d . |[5]
                                    [s]

However, some verses are quite short as they stand:

149: s í d r a s ó r g a | f ó r ð a m   w é a r ð |
                                [s e c g u m]

Eight of the twenty-one long lines that the editors emend because there apparently is no alliteration present in the manuscript reading have words beginning with an /h/ alliterating with vowels.[6] In every case the /h/ precedes a vowel also. The suggestion that the sound likeness actually present when vowels alliterate is that of the glottal stops which precede the vowels leads me to the following speculation: by the tenth century, /h/ may have represented the kind of aspirated sound that gave the vowels following them a likeness to the glottal stop preceding the vowels. In other words, if vowels could alliterate with each other, then the vowels following an /h/ would be as much like them as they were like each other. If this could be the case, then it seems to me that when the editors delete the very clearly drawn *h*s from the text they are denying their readers information about the OE language in the tenth century. *Hunferþ* and *hond* (also spelled *hand* and always the first element of a compound) account for seven of the emendations. Examples of each and of the other h-word emended are as follows:

  499: Hún ferð   máþelode | écglafes   béarn
2929: éald 7éges   full | hónd   slyht   agéaf |[7]
  332: óret mécgas | æfter   hǽleþum   frǽgn ‖

A line that may lend support to the proposal just suggested is 312. In it the editors add an /h/ to provide alliteration:

312: him   þa hílde   déor | [h]óf módigra |

Scragg's article provides the best summary I have found of what has been done to trace the phonetic change in /h/ from OE to ME, and also to tabulate the occurrences of *h* alliterating with vowels in the OE Poetic Codices. If his description of the instability of *h* can be used to support the above hypothesis, I suggest that the alliteration pattern in a number of other lines would also be changed to become in some cases a a a x (as in 2358 and in 1571: *éfne   swa   of   héfene | hádre   scineð*) and in others double-cross patterns (as in 897 and in 2000: *þæt is ún dýrne | drýhten hígelac*). And in line 84 the necessity for emendation would be eliminated, and instead there would be a double-cross pattern of b a a b in a line that is now assumed to have no alliteration in the manuscript:

> 84: þætse sécg   héte | áþum   swérian
> [ʃ]

The phoneme /h/ was apparently always unstable in OE, and doubtless had also a certain ambiguity in alliterating qualities if the above proposition holds, because it continued to alliterate in other ways: for example, in a double-cross pattern in contrast with vowels, as in 1182, 2973, and in 3164: *éall swylce   hýrsta | swylce on hórde ǽr;* but then also in contrast with itself, so to speak, for in line 1151 /h/ with a vowel forms a double-cross pattern with /h/ with a consonant.

> 1151: for   hábban   in hréþre#ða   wæs   héal hróden |

However, this contrast is not maintained elsewhere, for the many examples of /h/ alliterating with /h/ show a disregard as to whether /h/ is followed by a vowel or by one of the four consonants with which it clusters—/hw/ /hr/ /hl/ and /hn/. But if in line 1151 above there is not a contrast, then we have a case of four alliterating stresses (a a a a) in a long line—that is, alliteration in the final stress position of the meter.

There are just a few other long lines in *Beowulf* with four alliterations. All depend on a change in previous readings of the lines. For example, the following changes the usual C type reading of the b-verse:

> 1772: ǽscum   7 écgum | þæt íc me   ǽnigne

And line 3148 would have four alliterating stresses if one accepts /h/ alliterating with a vowel:

> hát on hréðre | hígum   únrote

On the other hand, there are other verses with the second or third

alliteration occurring on the final stress position. One has been retained by
Klaeber and by Wrenn to form the interesting pattern x a a a:

   574: hwǽþere   mege   sǽlde | þæt ic mid swéorde   of slóh |

Others have been emended. In line 2916 the /h/ of *gehnægdon* is dropped
on the pretext of better sense, although a meaning, and perhaps a more
poetic one, can be read in the original line:

   2916: þær hyne   hét wáre | hílde ge hnǽgdon |

In the other, two emendations are made as follows:

   2523: r é ð e s 7h á t t r e s | f o r ð o n i c me ó n   h á f u |
         [o]   [ɧ]

Of course, with the emendation we would have four alliterating stresses if
we accept *h* with a vowel alliterating with the vowels.

   Perhaps lines such as the foregoing attest only to the possibility of the
final stress position entering into the alliteration pattern, and then perhaps
only, as Baum suggested, to honor the rule in the breach (p. 156).

THE REMAINDER

A number of other verses in *Beowulf* have been classified in different ways
by various metricists. Some are probably poetically unsuccessful. I would
hesitate to call them unmetrical until I have confidence that we understand better than we do now what rhythmical variations the OE meter
could tolerate within its basic pattern.[8] Since any proposal that attempts to
describe this tolerance principle should be subjected to the historically
difficult lines, I offer the following readings. I give Bliss's and Pope's
classifications to the right of each verse for purposes of comparison, and
provide a few comments.

x́x x́x x̀ x | 2435b: únge   défelìce | rem (F)
12 12 1 2 3   '   '   '

xx x́x x x́x   414a: under   héofenes   hádor   emd (F)
12 12 3 12   '   '   '

x́x x́x x̀ x   2297a: éalne   útan   wèard ne#   hyp (F)
12 12 1 2   '   '   '

The types I see in these verses are clear from the distribution of the stress
marks over the four members in the abstract pattern at the left.

Those lines involving the gerunds which have received so much discussion seem to me also to measure into recognizable patterns. In these verses we encounter the same alternatives for handling three syllables before a line break when the following verse begins with an ictus that we discussed before. Only 1941a is so affected.

| x́x xx x́ xx | 473a: Sórh is me̦ to sécganne \| | A (D*) |
| 12 12 1 23 | | |

| x́x xx x́ xx | 1941a: ídese̦   to éfnanne ‖ | 1A* (D*) |
| 12 12 1 23 | | |

| \|x x́ xx x́ xx | 2093a: \| To lǎng ys to réccenne | rem (D*) |
| 12 1 23 1 23 | | |

Since the question of the quantity of *getawum* has caused the disagreement in the classification of the following three verses, my measurement (which does not recognize quantity as creating a 2:1 ratio between syllables) will not answer the objections. But I would measure them as follows:

| xx x́x x́ x \| | 368a: hy on wíg ge táwum \| | d4 (B1) |
| 12 12 1 2 3 | | |

| xx xx x́x x́x \| | 2636a: þæt we him ða gúð ge táwa \| | d4 (B1) |
| 12 12 12 12 3 | | |

The third verse of this group is always emended since it makes no semantic sense as the scribe wrote it. (I put the offending *a* in parentheses.)

| \| x xx x́x x́ x | 395b: \| in eowrum   gúð ge(a)tá wum | d4 (B1) |
| 1 2 12 12 1 2 | \| | |

REALIZATION RULES AMPLIFIED

The summary that may be drawn from the measurement process demonstrated first in chapter iii in long lines, then in the Five Types of Sievers, and finally in the verses that have always raised questions, may be stated as an amplification of the *Abstract and Realizations Rules* I proposed first on p. 53. I will conclude the summary with a measurement of a body of verse from *Beowulf* taken from different parts of the poem.

Abstract pattern rules
        1. OE meter is of that kind which patterns the recurrence of
           phrase stresses in short, phrasal line units.

2. OE meter is a pattern of two phrase stresses in a four member verse.

Realization rules
  A. Regarding the members:
    1. A member is typically constituted by a syllable.
    2. The syllable of any and all of the four members may generate a measure.
    3. A syllable in a member-position may be displaced by a word-boundary pulse.
    4. A word- or phrase-boundary pulse may initiate or complete a measure in any member-position.

  B. Regarding the phrase stresses:
    5. The two phrase stresses may occur on any two of the four members, thus creating any one of six possible patterns: x́xx́x, x́xx́x, xx́x́x, x́xx́x, x́xx́x, xxx́x́.
    6. Four-member, two phrase-stress verses are linked together into long lines by means of alliteration.
    7. Alliteration may occur with any two or more of the four phrase stresses in a long line, but normally not on the final one unless in a double, transverse pattern.

  C. Regarding the line breaks:
    8. The breaks between verses are heard as phrase-boundary pulses.
    9. Line breaks may constitute a full measure of time heard as a pause.
    10. The line-break pulses may complete a measure begun in the preceding verse, or may begin a measure that is completed in the following verse, or may constitute one pulse in a measure that bridges the two verses.
    11. The full measure begun in the line break may include a syllable of the following verse, which constitutes one of the four members in that verse.
    12. If a verse has four members with an additional upbeat syllable that is part of the measure begun in the line break, the line break measure apparently does not break the rule limiting a verse to four members.

In the lines that follow I indicate the four members by separating the x's in the abstract pattern. The phrase-stress marks show the type I see in the verse, although I do not provide an identifying letter. I do not because of the ambiguity that exists among Sievers' Five Types, which is emphasized in verses of five and six syllables, where the assignment of the four members often becomes very arbitrary. I am usually guided by the type label assigned by Sievers and Pope, perhaps only in an effort to be as conservative as possible in order to prevent showing too many as not conforming. At the same time, I consider this essential ambiguity among Sievers' types as indicative of their weakness as a statement of OE meter.

FROM THE PROLOGUE

x̆ ‖ x x́+ x́ x | x x́+ x́ x |
1 2 3 12 1 2 1 2 12 1 2 3

HWÀET   WE   GÁRDÉ na. | ingéar dágum.

x́+ x́ x̀ x | x́ x x́ x |
12 1 2 1 2 1 2 1 2 3

þéod   cýnìnga | þrým   ge frúnon |

xx x́x x́ x | x́ x x́x x #
12 12 1 2 3 1 2 12 312

huða   æþe língas | éllen   fré medon. #

x x́+ x́ x | x́x x x́ x |
3 12 1 2 3 12 3 1 2 3

Oft scýl scéfing | scéaþena þréatum |

5

x́x x x́ x | x́x x̀x x x́ ‖
12 3 1 2 3 12 12 3 123

mónegum mǽgþum | méodo sètla of téah ‖

x́ x̀ x x́ | xx x́ x x́ |
1 2 3 1 2 12 1 2 1 2

égsode éorl | syððan ǽrest wéarð. |

x́ x x́ x # xx x́ xx x́ ‖
1 2 1 231 23 1 23 1 23

féa sceaft fúnden # he þæs frófre gebád. ‖

x́ xx x́ x | x́ x̀ x x́ |
1 23 1 2 3 1 2 3 1 2

wéox under wólcnum | wéorð mỳndum þáh

x́ xx x́ x | xx x́+ x́ xx |
1 23 1 2 1 23 12 1 23 1

óð þæt him æghwylc | þara ýmb sítten dra |

10

xx x́+ x́ x | x́ x x́ x |
23 12 1 2 3 1 2 1 2 3

ofer hrón   ráde | hýran scólde |

x́ x x́ x # xx x́+ x́ x #
1 2 1 231 23 12 1 2 12

gómban gýldan # þæt wæs gód cýning. #

x x́x x x́ | x́ x x́ x |
3 12 3 1 2 1 2 1 2 3

ðæm éafera wæs | æfter cénned |

x́ x x́ x | xx x́+ x́ x |
1 2 1 2 1 23 12 1 2 3

géong ingéardum | þone gód sénde |

x́ xx x́ x # x́x x̀x x x́ | fólce tofrófre # fýren ðeàrfe   on   géat |
1 23 1 212 12 12 3 1 2

15

xx x́+ x́ x | x́ x x́ x | þæt hie   ǽr drúgon | áldor *lé*ase. |
12 12 1 2 3 1 2 1 2 3

x́ x x́ x # x x x x́+ x́ | lánge hwíle # him þæs líf fréa |
1 2 1 212 1 2 12 1 2
          xx x́ + x́ |

x́ x x́ x | x́x x̀x x x́ #   wúldres   wéa l dend | wórold àre for géaf. #
1 2 1 2 3 12 12 3 123

x́ xx x́ x ‖ x́+ x́ x x̀ | béowulf wæs bréme ‖ blǽd wíde spràng |
1 23 1 212 12 1 2 1 2

x́ x x́x x | x́x x̀ x x x́ #   scýldes éafera | scéde làndum ín. #
1 2 12 1 2 12 1 2 123

20

xx x́+ x́ x | x́x x x́ x | Swa sceal *géong* gúma | góde ge wýr cean |
12 12 1 2 3 12 3 1 2 3

x́x x́ x̀ x | x x́x x́ x | frómum   féoh gìftum. | on fǽder *béa*rme |
12 1 2 3 1 2 12 1 2 1

x x́x x x́x | x́ x x́x x | þæt híne on ýlde | éft ge wúni gen |
2 12 3 12 3 1 2 12 1 2

x́ x x́ x | xx x́+ x́ x | wíl gesíþas | þonne wíg cúme. |
1 2 1 2 1 23 12 1 2 3

x́ xx x́ x # x́ x̀ x x x́ | léode ge lǽsten # lóf dǽdum   scéal |
1 23 1 212 1 2 3 1 2

x x́ xx x̀x | x́ x x́ #   25
3 1 23 12 3 1 2 1 23   in mǽgþa ge hwǽre | mán ge þéon. #

MEDITATIVE DISCOURSE

1724

    # x́x xx x́ xx | # wúndor is to sécgan ne |
    12 12 1 23 1

x x́ x x́ | x́ x x́ x | hu míhtig gód | mán na cynne
2 1 2 1 2 1 2 1 2 1

x x́x x́ x | x́ x x́ x | þurh sídne séfan | snýttru   brýt tað |
2 12 1 2 3 1 2 1 2 3

x́x x́ x̀ x # xx x́ xx x́ #   éard 7éorl scìpe # he ah éalra ge wéald. #
12 1 2 312 12 1 23 123

x́x xx x́ x | x́ x x́ x |
12 12 1 2 3 1 2 1 2 3
hwīlum   he on lúfan | lǽteð   hwórfan |

x́x x́ x x̀ | x́ x x́ x |
12 1 2 1 2 1 2 1 2 3
mónnes mód ge þònc | mǽran cýnnes. |

1730
x́x xx x́ x | x́ x x́ x |
12 12 1 2 3 1 2 1 2 1
Séleð   him on éþle | éorþan wýnne |

x x́+ x́ x | x́ x̀ x́ x #
2 12 1 2 3 1 2 1 231
to héal dánne | hléo bùrh wéra #

x x̀x xx x́+ xx | x́x x x́ x |
2 12 12 12 12 3 12 3 1 2 3
ge dèð him swạ ge wéal déne | wórolde dǽlas |

x́ x x́ x | x xx x́ xx x́ |
1 2 1 2 1 2 12 1 23 1 2
síde ríce | þæt he his sélfa   ne mǽg |

xx x́+ x́ x | x́ xx x́ x #
12 12 1 2 3 1 23 1 2 12
for his ún snýttrum | én de ge þén cean. #

1735
x́x xx x́ x | xxx x́+ x́ x |
12 12 1 2 3 123 12 1 2 3
wúnað he on wíste | nọ hine   wíht dwéleð |

x́x x x́ x | xx x́ x x́ |
12 3 1 2 3 12 1 2 1 2
ádl ne ýldo | ne him ín wit sórh |

x x́x x́ x | xx x́x x́ x |
3 12 1 2 3 12 12 1 2 3
onséfað swéor ceð | nẹge sácu   óhwær |

x́ x̀x x́ x | xx x́+ x́ x |
1 23 1 2 3 12 12 1 2 3
écg hète éoweð | ac him éal wórold |

x́ xx x́ x # xx x́ xx x́ #
1 23 1 2 31 23 1 23 123
wén deð on wíllan # he þæt wýrse ne cón. #

XXV

1740
x́x xx x́ x | x́x x̀ x x́ |
12 12 1 2 3 12 1 2 1 2
Óð þæt him on ín nan | ófer hỳgda dǽl |

x́ xx x́ x | xxx x́+ x́ x |
1 23 1 2 3 123 12 1 2 3
wéaxeð 7wrídað | þonne se wéard swéfeð |

x́x x x́ x ‖ xx x́ x x́ |
12 3 1 212 12 1 2 1 2
sáwele hýrde ‖ bið se slǽp to fǽst |

x́ xx x́ x | x́x x̀ x x́ |
1 23 1 2 3 12 1 2 1 2
bís gum ge búnden | bóna   swiðe néah |

xxx x́+ x́ x | x́x x x́ x #
123 12 1 2 3 12 3 1 2 12

seþe of flán bógan | fýrenum scéo teð #

x́x xx x́ x | xx x́+ x́ x |
12 12 1 2 3 12 12 1 2 3

þónne bið on hréþre | under hélm drépen |

x́x x x́ x ‖ xx x́ xx x́ |
12 3 1 231 23 1 23 1 2

bíteran stræle ‖ him be béor gan ne cón |

x́+ x́ xx x̀x | x́ x x́ x #
12 1 23 12 3 1 2 1 2 12

wóm wún dor be bòdum | wér gan gástes #

x́x xx x́ x | x xx x́ x x́ ‖
12 12 1 2 1 2 12 1 2 123

þinceð him t o l ý tel | þæt he to lánge   héold ‖

x́x x́+ x̀ x | xxx x́+ x́ x |
12 12 1 2 3 123 12 1 2 3

gýt sað gróm   hydig | nall as   on gýlp séleð |

1750
x́ x x́ x # x xx x́ x x́ |
1 2 1 231 2 12 1 2 1 2

fædde béagas # 7he þa fórð ge scéaft |

x x́x xx x́ x | xx xx x́+ x́x |
3 12 12 1 2 3 12 12 12 12 3

for gýteð   7for gýmeð | þæs þe him ær gód séalde

x́ x x́ x | x́ x̀ x x́ #
1 2 1 2 3 1 2 3 123

wúldres wáldend | wéorð mỳnda dæl. #

xx x́ x x́ | x́ x x́ x |
12 1 2 1 2 1 2 1

hit on énde stæf | éft ge límpeð |

xx x́+ x́ x | x́x x x́ x |
23 12 1 2 3 12 3 1 2 3

þæt se líc hóma | læne ge dréoseð |

1755
x́x x x́ x # x́ x̀ x x́ |
12 3 1 2 121 2 3 1 2

fæge ge féalleð # féhð òþer tó |

xxx x́+ x́ x | x́ x x́ x |
123 12 1 2 3 1 2 1 2 3

seþe un múrn líce | mád mas dæl eþ |

x́x x́ x x̀ | x́x xx x́ x #
12 1 2 1 2 12 12 1 231

éorles ær ge strèon | égesan ne gýmeð. #

x x́x xx x̀x x̀ | x́ x x́ x |
2 12 12 12 1 2 1 2 1 2 3

be béor h þe ðone béalo nìð | béowulf léofa |

x́+x́ x | x xx x́ xx x́ |
1 2 1 2 1 2 12 1 23 1 2

sécg bétsta | 7þe þæt sélre   ge céos |

1760
x́ x x́ x # x́x x̀ xx x́ |
1 2 1 212 12 1 23 1 2

éce rædas # ófer hỳda ne gým |

x́ x x́ x #   xx xx x́x x́ | mǽra   cémpa # nu is þines   mǽgnes   blǽd |
1 2 1 2 12 12 12 12 1 2

x́ x x́ x | x́ x̀ x x́ | áne   hwíle | éft   sòna   bíð |
1 2 1 2 3 1 2 3 1 2

xx x́x xx x́ | x́x xx x́ x | þæt   þec   ádl   oððe   écg | éafoþes   ge twǽfeð |
12 12 12 1 2 12 12 1 2 3

xx x́ x x́ | xx x́ x x́ | oððe   fýres   féng | oððe   flódes   wýlm |
12 1 2 1 2 12 1 2 1 2

1765

xx x́x x́ x | xx x́ x x́ | oððe   grípe   méces | oððe   gáres   flíht |
12 12 1 2 3 12 1 2 1 2

xx x́x x́ x | xx x́x x x́x | oððe   átol   ýldo | oððe   éagena   béarhtm |
12 12 1 2 3 12 12 3 12 1

x x́x xx x́ x #   x́ x̀ x x́ | forsíteð   7for swórceð # sém ninga   bíð. |
2 12 12 1 2 12 1 2 3 1 2

x x+ x́+ x́ x | x́ xx x́ x #   þæt ðec drýht   gúma | déað ofer   swýðeð #
3 12 12   1 2 3 1 23 1 2 12

THE FINAL DIRGE

3169

xxx x́+ x́ x | x́ x x́ x | þaymbe   hlǽw   ríodan | hílde   déore |
123 12 1 2 3 1 2 1 2 3

x́x x̀ x x́ | x́ x x́ x | ǽþelìnga   béarn | éalra   twélfa |
12 1 2 1 2 1 2 1 2 3

xx x́x x́ x | x x́x x́ x | woldon   *céare*   cwíðan | 7cýning   mǽnan |
12 12 1 2 1 2 12 1 2 3

x́ x x́ x | xx x́+ x́ x || wórd gyd wrécan | 7ymb   wér   sprécan ||
1 2 1 2 1 23 12 1 2 12

x́xx x́ x̀ x | xx x́ x x́ #   éahtodan   éorl   scìpe | 7his éllen   wéorc #
123 1 2 3 1 23 1 2 123

x́x x x́ x | x xx x́x x́ | dúguðum   démdon | swa hit   ge*défe*   bíð |
12 3 1 2 1 2 12 12 1 2

x xx x́x x́ x | x́ x x́ x | þæt mon his wíne drýhten | wórdum   hérge |
3 12 12 1 2 3 1 2 1 2 3

x́ x x́ x | xxx x́+ x́ x | férhðum   fréoge | þonne he fórþ scíle |
1 2 1 2 3 123 12 1 2 1

x x́+ x́ x | x́ x x́ x #   oflíc háman | *lǽded*   wéorðan #
2 12 1 2 3 1 2 1 2 12

x́x x́ x̀ x ‖ x́ x x́ x | swá   begnórnodon ‖ géata   léode |
12 1 2 312 1 2 1 2 3   ˌ   ˌ   ˌ   ˌ

x́ xx x́ x | x́ x x́ x #   hláfordes *hrý*re | héorð genéatas #
1 23 1 2 3 1 2 1 2 12   ˌ   ˌ   ˌ   ˌ

                                            3180
x́x xx x́ x | x́x x́ x̀ x ‖   cwǽdon þæt he wǽre | wýruldcýni*nga* |
12 12 1 2 3 12 1 2 3 12   ˌ   ˌ   ˌ   ˌ

x́ x x́ x | x x́+ x́ x | *m*ánna   míldust | 7*món*   *þwǽr*ust |
1 2 1 2 1 2 12 1 2 3   ˌ   ˌ   ˌ   ˌ

x́ x x́ x | x x́+ x́ x #   léodum   líðost | 7lóf   géornost. #
1 2 1 2 1 2 12 1 2 12   ˌ   ˌ   ˌ   ˌ

Reference Matter

APPENDIX: THE ACCENTS AND POINTS
OF THE BEOWULF MANUSCRIPT

Two kinds of markings appear infrequently but consistently throughout the *Beowulf* manuscript, that of points between words within the lines and that of interlinear accent marks over words.[1] No conclusive theory concerning these markings has been developed, and probably none ever will be. But their presence in the manuscript is a constant reminder that they served some function; and their defiance of an association with syntactic units, on the one hand, or with long vowels on the other, removes the possibility that they are marks of punctuation or of classical quantity, and encourages an attempt to read them as metrical and rhythmical signs, used, as is evident from their scattered appearance, perhaps only when a reader might need help in giving a verse its correct intonation.

THE POINTS

There are some seven hundred points in *Beowulf*.[2] Somewhat over six hundred occur at the end of the long lines, some sixty at the end of verses, and thirteen within the verses. Because the overwhelming majority of them occur in relation to the one regular metrical unit in OE poetry, I think there can be little doubt that the points mark that metrical unit. They function like my line-break symbols (|, #), and their presence supports the fact that the scribe heard these boundaries.[3] The fact that he used the point only sporadically could reflect the habit of the oral tradition of his time (as seen in the chant manuscripts especially), which prompted scribes to call attention to something only if there was reason to think the reader (or chant master) might overlook it. This may also offer some expla-nation for the fact that both scribes, but especially the second, used the points more frequently toward the beginning of his work. After a while he too heard the line break so easily that he unconsciously decided any reader would do likewise. Further, the fact that fewer than ten percent of these end-of-verse marks occur after the a-verse supports the fact that the metrical framework in OE practice is that of long lines made up of two verses, rather than simply of verses.

Thirteen of the points, however, do not occur at the end of either verse or long line. But they do occur in places within the verses where there is a natural caesura—one of rhythmical significance.[4] Ten are in the position so assigned by Bliss: 61a, 279a, 423a, 553b, 1159a, 1974a, 1039a, 2673b, 2832b, and 2897a. In line 1039, for example, the point testifies to the reality of a caesura which Bliss grants only hypothetically because of the weighty interpretation he places on compounds. The manuscript reads thus:

xx x́ x+ x́x | 1039a: þæt   wæs   h í l d e ·   s é t l |
12 1 23 12 3

And in lines 61a and 2673b, the point seems to me also to heighten the rhythmical
nuances: in the latter, it may point up a caesura that initiates an extra measure:

x́x +x x́ x | 2673b: b ý r n e · n e m é a h t e |
12 12 1 2 3

Perhaps in this case it insures the clear separation of *-ne* and *ne-*; in the former, its
use prompts me to read thus:

x́x x+x x́+ x | 61: héoro   gàr · 7hróð   gàr | 7hálga   tíl |
12 123 12 1 2

or, perhaps equally dramatically, thus:

x́xx +x x́ x   héoro   gàr · 7hróð   gar | 7hálga   tìl |
123 12 1 2

   Three of the points within verses are not in a position assigned by Bliss for a
caesura, two because they are in light verses which do not command a caesura in
Bliss's system. But there is no doubt that in all three cases the natural speech
rhythm of the syntax is heightened by a rhythmical lengthening where these
points occur. This suggests that when the points do occur within verses they
probably command a full pulse. For if the scribe (mistakenly or purposely) used
a point, it is at least reasonable to assume that he heard the same kind of
boundary pulse here that he heard between verses and long lines, since that is
where they usually occurred. For example:

x x́+ xx x́x | 2542a: # g e s é a h ·   ð a   b e   w é a l l e |
123 12 12 12 3

In the following verse, the speech rhythm will be better understood if the two
proximate verses are provided:

                                    # þuwást   g i f   h i t   í s |
x́x+ x́ x̀ x ‖   273a: swá   we.sóþl i c e ‖ s é c g a n   h ý r d o n #
123 1 2 3

Here, *soplice* by its position in the clause requires rhythmical separation from the
surrounding words. Perhaps the scribe had mistakenly left no space, and later
inserted the point to counteract his omission. Perhaps in the following verse the

point was used to offset the habit of running *to pæs pe* together,

xx+ xxx x́xx x́ | 1585b: toðæs ·   þe he   onrǽste   ge séah |
123 123 123 1 2   '   + '   '   '

thus assuring the correct syntactical emphasis.

  One other point is brought within a verse by Wrenn's division of lines 1980b–1981a:

meodu   scencum |

hwearf · geond þæt side reced | hæreðes dohtor |

But this division is unusual among editions, and I consider the presence here of the point, in view of the preponderance of its use at the end of lines, to be of sufficient significance to invalidate Wrenn's treatment, and to do so without the necessity of providing another alliterating word for the poet.

THE ACCENT MARKS

There are 153 accent marks in the *Beowulf* manuscript according to the list provided by Dobbie. They vary in shape from the stub-end of a mark to a long and graceful *virgule*-like line. They usually extend (or did) over more than one letter, and sometimes more conspicuously over the consonant than over the vowel before it. They have been variously interpreted, usually not wholly acceptably because too many exceptions to a given thesis always weakened the rule proposed. Two of the most plausible attempts at interpretation provided in recent years, it seems to me, are those by Joynes and Nist in the same works in which they interpreted the points. Nist's proposal may be acceptable just because of its breadth—"the general meaning of the acute accent is 'special attention needed here'"—for he suggests that it distinguishes between homographs, marks relatively unusual alliteration and rhyme situations, sometimes marks the ends of lines and indicates the placing of primary and secondary stresses, and emphasizes the hypotactic flow of the syntax from line to line.[5] Joynes, on the other hand, sees a connection between the vast majority of the accent marks (as well as of the points) and juncture morphemes, and suggests that if this interpretation is true, "manuscript and metrical evidence consistently support the theory that the basic principle of Old English metrics was regularization of juncture morphemes."[6]

  The results of my own analysis of the accent marks lean in the direction of Joynes's conclusion, although I have abandoned the use of the structuralists' terms. And the fact that my approach was that of the rhythmist while hers was that of the linguist perhaps strengthens both our results, although I will express mine in somewhat different terms. Since stress, prominence, and word and phrase boundaries have shown themselves to be the determining elements in the meter and the rhythmical variations I find operating in *Beowulf,* I have catalogued the accent marks according to their relation to these prosodic features. I will simply report the statistics of that cataloguing process (with examples) and propose some very tentative conclusions. I am assuming the presence of all the marks as listed in Dobbie, although a number of them are questionable. In other words, assuming they are present, this is how they are catalogued. By the same process of reasoning, I am including one mark noted by Zupitza (897b) not found in Dobbie's list. This makes my working number 154. The type letters are from Bliss's list.

Table 1:   Accent Marks in Relation to Stress

On a Phrase Stress		On Secondary Stress	
Preceding the line break (|) 49		Preceding the line break (|) 15	
Type B	31	Type A	9
Type E	15	Type D	6
Type C	3		
Preceding another phrase stress: 22		Preceding a phrase stress: 5	
Type D	5	Type A	5
Type C	17		
Preceding a secondary: 23		Preceding a weak stress: 2	
Type A	11	Type E	2
Type D	6	*Totals*	22
Type E	5		
Type B	1	In Anomalous Positions	
		Preceding a Phrase Stress: 6	
Preceding a weak stress: 32		Type A	1
		Type B	2
Type A	21	Type C	2
Type B	11	Type D	1
Totals	126	*Total*	6

Two sets of figures in the above chart stand out: those showing the incidence of accent marks on the phrase stresses of the meter, and those occurring in conjunction with the line break. One hundred twenty-six (or 82 percent) occur on the phrase stress, and twenty-two (or 14 percent) on a secondary. The six (or 4 percent) anomalous marks seem principally to be over weak stresses; in some of these cases, their similarity to other accent-mark situations makes the traditional classification of these as weak stresses less tenable than is usually assumed. Sixty-four (or 43 percent) of the accent marks appear on the last syllable of a verse before a line break which always takes one or two counts. In view of this fact, it may be helpful to chart the coincidence of the remaining ninety with Bliss's caesura, before investigating further possible relationships of the accent mark to word and phrase boundaries.

Table 2:   Accent Marks Coinciding with Bliss's Caesura

On a Phrase Stress		On Secondary Stress	
Phrase stress + phrase stress: 22(22)		Secondary + phrase stress: 4(5)	
Phrase stress + secondary:	0(23)	Secondary + weak:	2(2)
Phrase stress + weak:	29(32)		
Type A	19(21)	In Anomalous Positions:	0(6)
Type B	10(11)		
Totals	51(77)		6(13)

Fifty-seven (or 63 percent of the ninety not occurring before the line break) occur on the syllable preceding Bliss's caesura. Since these figures added to the ones related to line breaks give us a total of one hundred twenty-one (or 79 percent) of the marks, they seem significant in relating the accent marks to a boundary (as well as to stress and prominence), and conversely in supporting in most cases the accuracy of Bliss's placement of the caesura. Of these fifty-seven, twenty-two occur in a position between two juxtaposed phrase stresses where a full count is always demanded to complete the measure after the first stress (regardless of accent mark), as we saw demonstrated so often above in our treatment of D and C types. Concerning the others, as we noted also in our analysis by types, the caesura as a rhythmic phenomenon is probably always present as a (+) boundary in the verses; hence its presence may become prominent enough in situations other than between two phrase stresses to demand its receiving a full beat. It would not then be difficult to accept as an assumption the suggestion that the scribe used a mark over such syllables when he heard the rhythmical lengthening that concurred with these syllables, that is, with the boundary, especially if such lengthening occurred in unlikely situations which might be overlooked by a reader. Since the "unlikeliness" of the situation depended on the scribe's judgment, it is difficult and probably impossible to determine why he used the mark in one place and not in another.

If we can accept some relationship between the accent mark and word and phrase boundaries in 121 of the 154 instances of its use, our major task is to discover any such relationship in the 32 remaining verses. This task can take on two aspects in view of the data on the second chart. Two categories show no coincidence with Bliss's caesura (one being the anomalous group), and it can be assumed that any boundary to which they may be related will not be a syntactical caesura. But in two other categories only a few (four in all) of the total number do not coincide; hence, the question may rather be whether Bliss erred in placing his caesura in these four instances. We will treat these four and the six anomalous verses individually, while giving only typical examples (and listing the line references in footnotes) from the other categories, taking them in turn as listed on the first chart.

An accent mark occurs on a phrase stress before | in forty-nine instances very similar to the following:

xxx x́ x x́ #   1883b: seþe   on   áncre   ra͡d #   B
123 1 2 123

x́x x̀ x x́ | 301b: flóta   stìlle   ba͡d | E
12 1 2 1 2

x x x́+ x́ | 2166b: swa sceal   mǽg + do͡n. | C
1 2 12 1 2

Of the forty-nine, only nine occur in the a-verse, which may support a theory saying that the accent mark also functions in calling attention to a nonalliterating stress in this final position.[7]

On one phrase stress that precedes another, the accent mark appears in such D and C types as the following:

x́+ x́ x̀ x   2716b: wi͡s + hýcgende   D
12 1 2 3

| x x́+ x́ x | 2090b: | gedo͡n + wólde | C
1 2 12 1 2

Eight of the seventeen occurrences of an accent mark in this position of a C type are on verses Bliss reclassified as d2 and d3, such as the following:

| x x́+ x́ x   1325a: | min ru͡n + wíta   C
1 2 12 1 2

I suggest that the accent mark in these cases supports the rereadings of these as authentic C types, since its presence, by analogy to other verses where it appears, strengthens the choice of the second stress position for beginning a new measure.[8]

It is in the next group (phrase stress + secondary) that we encounter our largest number of verses in which the accent mark bears no relationship to Bliss's caesura. These are the twenty-three accents on a phrase stress which precedes a secondary stress. This situation will be recognized as occurring most normally in D and E type verses, although the greatest number bearing accents are of type A. In reverse order, then, typical examples and my suggested reading of them along the guidelines found useful in chapters iii and iv above are the following:

x́+ x̀ x x́ #   564b: sæ͡ + grùnde   néah #   E
12 1 2 123

x́x x́+ x̀ x | 449a: éteð a͡ngèn ga | D
12 12 1 2 3

Perhaps in the latter the scribe used the accent mark to offset the fact that he had not spaced before the following secondary stress, as he does in most of these cases when the secondary stress initiates a new measure. Another of the type D verses with an accent mark perhaps supports our acceptance of three-syllable verses:

x́+ x́+ x̀ #   1546a: brád + brûn + ècg #   D
12 12 1 23

In these E and D types, it is not so difficult to accept a (+) boundary taking a full count, because we have seen it do so with ease before in a number of other such lines. When the same situation occurs in a type A verse, however, we may be reluctant to give it the extra full count; but if the accent mark usually denotes a rhythmical lengthening by means of a boundary pulse, it can also do so without force in such cases as the following:

x́ xx x́+ x | 33a: ísig 7ût + fùs | A
1 23 12 1 2

And when the accent on a phrase stress before a secondary stress occurs early in the verse, the secondary is always followed by an unstressed syllable to avoid what might be otherwise an awkward metrical situation.

x́+ xx x́ x   1116a: bân + fàtu bǽr nan   A
12 12 1 x

One verse that I have grouped with these of type A belongs to the hypermetric verses:

x́+ xx x́xx xx   1168a: ār + fæ̀st   æt écga   gelàcum #   A
12 12 123 12

The rhythmical effect of this accent mark, it seems to me, also helps to disprove any theory that says the hypermetric lines are read twice as fast as normal lines. Two other accent marks on verses of type A and a single instance of type B fall into this category also:[9]

x́+ x x́ x | 1896b: sǽ + gèap náca | A
12 3 1 2 3

x́+ x x̀x x #   2043a: gár + cwèalm   gúmena #   A
12 3 12 3

| x xx x́+ x x́ | 537b: | þæt wit   on gár + sècg   út | B
1 2 12 12 3 1 2

However, they show a distinct difference from the others because the secondary stress does not in these cases take an ictus, but simply the third count of the

measure, and hence the degree of stress seems to be somewhat reduced rhythmically. Nevertheless, they are still closest to this class in that their accent marks
have no relation to Bliss's position of the caesura.[10]

All of the accents in this category (phrase stress + secondary), which have no
relation to Bliss's caesura and probably would not in any system, nevertheless
show an easy adaptation to a boundary pulse. Whether such a boundary always
has the value of a full pulse between the primary and secondary stresses may be
questioned. As I have tried to show by my demonstration, giving it a full beat is
preferable in many cases and assimilable without being awkward in others,
perhaps giving the verse a somewhat more dramatic rhythmic character. However, in the latter cases it seems to me that no hard and fast rule need be adopted.
If the accent mark indicates a rhythmical lengthening only, with a temporal value
of less than a full beat, this probably would not diminish the usefulness of the
mark (in the scribe's opinion) if he felt that a rhythmical lengthening of any value
at all needed to be recognized. He was not "counting" the measures.

Thirty-two accent marks occur over a phrase stress which precedes a weak
stress. This is the kind of situation where one least expects additional rhythmical
lengthening, since the weak stresses can complete the measure. However, because
the vast majority of these coincide with Bliss's caesura, the accent mark may well
support the validity of his placement of it. For example, all of the instances in
type A verses that so coincide belong to Bliss's 1A (that is, the caesura occurs
immediately after the phrase stress); and all of the type B verses that so coincide
belong to Bliss's 2B (which fits Sievers' caesura in the Bs also), as in the following:

x́+ xx x́ x	211a: bãt + under béorge #	1A1
12 12 1 2		
x́+ x x́ x	336a: ãr + 7óm biht #	1A1
12 3 1 2		
xx x́+ x x́ |	100b: oððæt ắn + ongán |	2B1
12 12 3 1 2		

As is evident in the abstract pattern given to the left of these verses, the metrical
handling of these accent marks is no different from that of the preceding group, in
spite of the fact that these concur with the caesura and the others do not. Like the
preceding group also, the value of the boundary pulse may be a relative one
rather than the full pulse we have given it for the sake of demonstration.[11]

The three verses in this category whose accent marks are at variance with Bliss's
caesura, are so for different reasons. One is a verse of type a1d (A3); to this type he
does not assign a caesura, which otherwise would probably fall naturally in the
position after the accent mark:

x́+x xx x́ x |	681a: nãt + he þara góda |	a1d
123 12 1 2 3		

The other two (one A and one B) are of an entirely different character since they involve two-syllable words carrying the accent. But because of the indefiniteness of the exact letter over which an accent mark appears, it is impossible to say whether the scribe meant for it to govern the entire word or simply the first long syllable. Either judgment is possible, and probably also acceptable. If the accent mark is thought of as acting over the entire word, then the following interpretation might be given:

x̀x +x x́ x | 2655a: fáne + gefýllan | 1A + 1a
12 12 1 2 3   ′   ′

xx x́ x+ x́#   2553b: under hárne + stán #   3B1b
12 1 23 123   ′   ′   ′

With such an interpretation, the accent mark may still be said to coincide with Bliss's caesura. On the other hand, since the first syllable of both words has a long vowel, it may be this rhythmical lengthening to which the scribe is calling attention. I would prefer this reading, although in 2655a it makes a (+) boundary with a full pulse somewhat awkward, and I thus offer alternatives:

x́+ xx x́ x | fáne gefýllan | fáne gefýllan | x̀x x x́ x |
12 12 1 2 3   +   ′   ′   ′   12 3 1 2 3

xx x́+ x x́#   2553b: under hárne stán #
12 12 3 123   ′   ′ +   ′

Only twenty-two of the accent marks are found on secondary stresses. Of these, the majority (fifteen) are on the last syllable of the verse with its (|) line break. However, the accent in this position may also serve to strengthen the secondary degree of this stress. For example, since they occur only in A and D verses, it seems to me all the verses should be classified as A2 (x́ x x́ x̀) or D4, 5, or 6 (x́ x́ x x̀). As a matter of fact, all but four are so classified, and I suggest that these four should be as well on the force of the accent mark which appears over them. Since there are no other questions in the reading of these verses where the line break simply takes the extra beat, I include here four typical examples, using one of the four from the A1 type which I suggest should also be A2.[12]

x́ x x́ x | 357a: éald 7ún hầr | 1A1a
1 2 1 2 3   ′   ′

x́ x x́ x #   2586a: íren ǽr gòd #   2A2
1 2 1 2   ′   ′

x́ x x̀x x#   2196a: bóld 7brégo stòl #   1A2a
1 2 12 123   ′   ′   ′

x́+ x́ x x#   210a: fýrst + fórð gewầt #   1D4
12 1 2 123   ′   ′   ′

Of the five instances of an accent mark appearing on a secondary stress preceding a phrase stress (all of type A), only one does not coincide with Bliss's caesura. One of the typical examples (from the four) is as follows: [13]

x́ x+x́ | 1275b: déaþ wíc + séon | 2A3a
1 2 3 1 2

The one accent mark not to coincide is the following:

x́x x+ x́ x   1388a: dómes æ̆r + déaþe #   1A + 1a
12 12 1 2

It seems to me that here the accent mark, by calling attention to *ær,* probably invests it with secondary stress (as Sievers also classifies it), and if at the same time it is lengthened by the boundary to another full pulse, it must also initiate a measure, as shown. I suggest, then, that rhythmically the boundary takes place with *ær,* not before it as Bliss's classification has it do.

Only two verses show an accent mark on a secondary stress before a weak, and both of these support Bliss's reading of the verses:

x́+ x̀+ x x́#   897b: wýrm + hằt + geméalt #   2E2a
12 12 3 123

x́x x̀+ x x́ | 3144b: wúd[u] rĕc + astáh | 2E2a
12 12 3 1 2

The six accent marks I have grouped together as anomalous occur principally on weak stresses preceding phrase stresses in the classifications to which they have been traditionally associated. The main factor they have in common is that none of them coincides with Bliss's caesura. However, other resemblances can be traced between a few of them, and these resemblances may offer some clues to their function. The six verses in which they occur are the following:

386b: (1)	hat	ingan			2C1a
1390a:	áris	rices	weard		1D5 with anacrusis
1371b:	ǽr	he	in	wille	2C1b
775b:	þær	fram	sylle	a beag	3B + 1b
264a:	gebad	wintra	worn		3B1b
1626a:	Eodon	him	þato geanes		ale

The easiest explanation is that these accent marks serve one or more of several purposes, and they may exhibit their relationship, if any, to stress, prominence, and boundaries either by calling attention to an unusual stress position (giving it prominence by adding a boundary pulse to it) or by giving the following syllable stress-prominence by supplying a boundary pulse before it.

Either hypothesis might be supported in regard to the first two examples (386b and 1390a). The traditional classifications for them (shown at the right) would support the second—that the accent mark adds a boundary pulse to the weak syllables, thereby giving prominence to the following phrase stresses. But, perhaps unfortunately, this is the hypothesis that finds least support from the other 148 accent marks which occur always with phrase stress or secondary stress. For this reason alone, I suggest the possibility of a radical reexamination of the verses, allowing the elements we saw operating in other verses to operate here too. In 386b, since the scribe used no spacing between *in* and *gan* and added attention with accent marks to the two words around *in,* and since 96 percent of the accent marks are on syllables generally accepted as exhibiting phrase stress or secondary stress, is it possible that the scribe heard a stress on *hat,*[14] making the verse an A type, rather than a C with *in* as the principal phrase stress? In other words, did he hear the following kind of rhythm and meter?

$$\acute{x} + x \ \acute{x} \ | \qquad\qquad 386b: \ \overset{\frown}{hat} + ing\overset{\frown}{an} \ |$$
$$1\,2\,3 \ \ 1 \ \ 2$$

This reading, of course, defies the rule of alliteration which says that vowels may not alliterate with *h-* (a rule to which we gave some attention in chapter v above). Such a rereading has already been given by Nist to the second verse under examination (1390a); Nist puts it in a group in which the accent mark is interpreted as indicating which of two possible alliterative systems in the line should be taken as primary, and reads it thus: "*Áris rices weard uton hraþe feran.*"[15] I find this also the *easiest* solution, because it attributes to these accent marks the same function as that which 96 percent of the others seem to have. I would add, however, that it may still retain in this verse an individual character in that the position of the mark (extending from approximately the middle of *a-* to well over *-r-*) suggests a rhythmical lengthening that perhaps colors both syllables, although I can demonstrate this on paper only by means of a + boundary between them:

$$\acute{x} + x \ \acute{x}x \ x \ | \qquad 1390a: \ \overset{\frown}{a}r\,i\,s \quad r\,i\,c\,e\,s \quad w\,e\,a\,r\,d \ | \ \acute{u}\,t\,o\,n \ -$$
$$1\,2\,3 \ \ 12 \ \ 1 \ 2 \qquad\qquad\qquad\qquad +$$

If there is an accent mark in our third example, 1371b, it will cause the verse to be read in the same way as the two verses we have just discussed. However, its presence is doubtful—it was noted only by Thorkelin A, and the facsimile shows nothing that resembles even the dimmer traces of other accent marks—too doubtful certainly for conjecturing a reclassification of the verse over which it is found.

The fourth example in our anomalous group would seem to indicate a caesural boundary, since the mark, ending right over *a-*, must originally have been begun in the center of the space before it. This would seem to make the verse fit neatly into the group of type B verses whose accent marks coincide with Bliss's caesura. But it does not fit neatly because all the verses in that group have the accent mark on a phrase stress *preceding* the caesura. It may seem even closer to the two type E verses (897b and 3144b) in which the caesura begins the new measure, but again, in those the accent is on the preceding secondary stress. Hence, reading the verse according to its accepted classification

xx x́x +x x́ | 775b: þǽr   fram   sýlle + ȃbéag | 3B + 1b
12 12 12 1 2   ꞈ   ꞈ ꞈ ꞈ

gives this accent mark a function unique among the 154 in the manuscript. Interpreting it, on the other hand, according to the general stress and boundary pattern of accent marks in the majority of lines, gives *abeag* the same treatment as *aris* in 1390a and makes the verse a type C, as follows:

xx x́x x́ x | 775b: þæ r   f r am   sýl l e   ȃbe ag |
12 12 1 2 3   ꞈ   ꞈ   +

However, I could accept this latter reading only if the accent mark did not in this instance indicate a full count (just as I did not give it the count in the pattern to the left).

The accent mark in 264a best fits our second conjecture concerning the function of these anomalous marks—that of giving the following word prominence by supplying a pulse before it. This hypothesis allows the retention of *gebad* as weak stresses before the phrase stress, *wintra,* in the B type. Again, such a reading gives a unique function to this mark, although there might be some common ground between it and verses 386b and 1390a, if the traditional readings of these are retained. In any case, at least in 264a, *gebad* cannot under any circumstances become one of the two primary stresses in the line. But, could not the accent mark still indicate for -*bad* something more than a weak stress, a condition that without some mark might be overlooked because there are two alliterating stresses in the verse. It would still read as a type B, but with this sort of rhythm:

#x x̀+ x́ x x́ | 264a: # gebȃd + wíntra   wórn |
123 12 1 2 1 2

And this seems perfectly natural, and perhaps also provides us with another insight for the interpretation of 386b: *hat ingan.* For both verses show accents over verbs standing first in their lines. Their position alone accords them stress. If the syllables following them are the first of the two primary stresses, then the accent marks may have been used to assure at least sufficient stress attention to these verbs. Perhaps the other two anomalous accent marks we have discussed (also over verbs, incidentally) also have the function of making their syllables secondary stresses, rather than leaving them as the traditional weak or lifting them to the radical primary. The boundary pulses with them would then still give to the following primary stresses the necessary rhythmical prominence. Such an interpretation would place these anomalous verses in the category of "secondary + phrase stress" and perhaps yet leave them in their traditional type classifications, though putting secondary stresses in rather unusual places for those types.

And the sixth verse of this group could be interpreted in a like manner—if it really has an accent mark. I find the character of the mark found over *to,* however, too unlike the authentic accent marks to support a conjecture.

There is one mark in the manuscript that seems never to be noticed by editors (probably because it is clearly over consonants), although, unless the facsimile is particularly deceiving, its presence seems particularly evident. It appears thus:

1344: se þe   eow   wel   hwylcr̃a | wilna   dohte.

and may indeed have somewhat the same rhythmical significance as the rest of the accent marks we have treated.

To complete in summary what was shown in the tables at the beginning of this section on the accents: these interlinear marks show a striking consistency in their appearance in conjunction with line breaks and caesuras, and with phrase stresses and intermediate stresses. All but the six anomalous marks (or 96 percent) appear over syllables traditionally recognized as bearing a phrase stress or secondary stress, and 79 percent of them occur over the syllables preceding either the end-of-verse line break or the within-the-verse caesura, which ordinarily take (or may take) a full pulse in their respective measures.

In our analysis of the 21 percent not occurring in conjunction with | or + boundaries, we found that one entire group (23: phrase stress preceding second-ary) could easily accommodate a boundary pulse since syllables in that position often do so whether they carry an accent mark or not, just as we found this in our analysis of the Five Types in chapter iv above. Of the four other accents not conforming to Bliss's caesura, two perhaps indicate that his positioning of the caesura may need reexamination, and the remaining two depend on the reading of the accent as being either over one or over both syllables of dissyllabic words. The inclusion of a boundary pulse would be awkward in neither interpretation.

Of the six anomalous verses only four were analyzed, because of the doubtful character of the other two marks. Three possible alternate readings were suggested: (1) Adherence to the traditional classification of these verses, which makes the accents to occur over weak syllables, causes these accents to function differ-ently from the other 96 percent, but even so they could indicate a boundary before or after the syllables over which they occur, perhaps in order to call attention to the phrase stresses which follow them. (2) A reinterpretation of three of the verses granting phrase stress to the syllables over which the accents occur is possible and would make these verses conform to the other 96 percent, but it would necessitate a radical reclassification of their types. (3) Perhaps a middle way is that of allowing the accent mark to indicate at least secondary stress, in which case the addition of the boundary pulse would then serve to heighten the rhythmical effect of the syllable in relation to the phrase stress following it.

An interpretation of the accent mark as bearing a connection to the line breaks, phrase stresses, caesuras and intermediate stress—rhythmical elements which determine the meter and provide the rhythmical variations of OE poetry—seems then a logical consequence of the theory proposed in this book. But more importantly, since my analysis of the accent marks preceded the clarification and application of principles of rhythm and meter and provided me with many of the clues that resulted in my analysis of *Beowulf,* it seems to me that the consistency found in the relationship of the accent marks to prominence and boundaries may also give manuscript support to the theory proposed.

NOTES

INTRODUCTION

1 "Meter and the Free Rhythm of *Beowulf,*" Diss. Notre Dame 1964.
2 Two articles were part of that effort: "Some Linguistic Criteria in the Accommodation of the English Mass Text to Sung Recitative and Melody," *Caecilia,* 91 (1964), 48–62; and "Adapting the Psalm Tones to English," *Liturgical Arts Quarterly,* 34 (1965), 7–12.
3 For example, see "Measuring the Rhythmic Variations of Old English Meter," *Language and Style,* 8 (1975), 95–110; and also a book review article, "Suprasegmentals, Meter, and the Manuscript of *Beowulf,*" *Linguistics,* 62 (1970), 110–17, and *A Prosody Manual: Rhythm and Meter in English Poetry,* printed for class use by Oklahoma State Univ., 1971.
4 Thomas Cable, *The Meter and Melody of Beowulf* (Urbana: Univ. of Illinois Press, 1974). Baum and Taglicht are documented in chapter 1.
5 A. J. Bliss, *The Metre of Beowulf* (Oxford: Basil Blackwell, 1958; 2nd ed. rev., 1967).
6 John C. Pope, *The Rhythm of Beowulf* (New Haven: Yale Univ. Press, 1942; 2nd ed. rev., 1966).
7 My definition owes its form particularly to John Lotz, "Metrics," *Current Trends in Linguistics,* ed. Thomas A. Seboek, No. 12 (The Hague: Mouton, 1974), 963–82, which is a reprint with additions (including my reference) of the introductory article in *Versification,* ed. W. K. Wimsatt (New York: Modern Language Association, 1972). Cf. also the seminal article of Wimsatt and Monroe C. Beardsley, "The Concept of Meter: An Exercise in Abstraction," *PMLA,* 74 (1959), 585–98. In relation to the whole subject of meter, recent articles by linguists that I have found partially satisfying and sometimes exciting are the following: Paul Kiparsky, "Stress, Syntax, and Meter," *Language,* 51 (1975), 576–616; G. Knowles, "The Rhythm of English Syllables," *Lingua,* 34 (1974), 115–47; and the following three in *Linguistics:* Ju. M. Lotman, "On Some Principle Difficulties in the Structural Description of a Text," 121 (1974), 57–63; E. A. Levensten, "A Scheme for the Inter-Relation of Linguistic Analysis and Poetry Criticism," 129 (1974), 29–47; and N. V. Lebedeva, "Certain Syntagmatic Features of Poetic Speech," 141 (1974), 35–42.

CHAPTER 1

1 See Thomas Cable, "Timers, Stressers, and Linguists: Contention and Compromise," *MLQ,* 33 (1972), 227–39.

2 *The Meter and Melody of Beowulf* (Urbana: Univ. of Illinois Press, 1974). Reference to this work will be cited in my text and notes as *MM* with page number.

3 *Linguarum vett. septentrionalium Thesaurus grammatico-criticus et archaeologicus* (Oxford, 1705), I, 177. (The times of which have toward those around them a ratio or apt proportion, composed from diverse times and movements in pleasing and appropriate measures.)

4 Lachmann presented his theory in a lecture, "Über das Hildebrandslied," before the Berlin *Akademie der Wissenschaften.* It was published in an essay, "Über althochdeutsche Betonung und Verskunst." Both titles, and another pertinent one, "Über Singen und Sagen," can be found in *Kleinere Schriften zur Deutschen Philologie,* I (Berlin, 1876). On Lachmann, see also Jakob Schipper, *A History of English Versification* (Oxford: Clarendon, 1910), pp. 16–21.

5 My authorities for these and any other of the following early theorists not referred to in my notes are Schipper, and Max Kaluza, *A Short History of English Versification,* trans. A. C. Dunstan (London: George Allen, 1911).

6 Eduard Sievers, "Zur Rhythmik des germanischen Alliterationsverses," *Paul and Braune's Beiträge,* 10 (1885), 209–314; and *Altgermanische Metrik* (Halle: M. Niemeyer, 1893).

7 *Zur althochdeutschen Alliterationspoesie* (Kiel, 1888). See also Kaluza, pp. 50–52.

8 John C. Pope, *The Rhythm of Beowulf,* 2nd ed., rev. (New Haven: Yale Univ. Press, 1966). John Nist, "The Metrics of Beowulf," *The Structure and Texture of Beowulf* (São Paulo, Brazil: Univ. of São Paulo Press, 1959), pp. 89–110. C. L. Wrenn, in his review of another book in *Review of English Studies,* 11 (1960), 415, commented that Nist presents "particularly well" this point of view of chanting in unequal phrases, "in modification of the Pope method of scansion," and adds that his study of metrics "merits close attention." However, it seems to me that there is a difference between what Nist says in print and his method of reading. His reading at the 1963 MLA meeting, for example, demonstrated a strict adherence to a heavy isochronous beat.

9 It seems to me that children's verse and nursery rhymes in English are in the tradition of the two-beat theory as Nist demonstrates it.

10 See also Pope's summary, p. 21. The numbers here are provided for easy reference later in showing the relation of Heusler's theory to Pope's.

11 Ten Brink's system was recorded fully by one of his students, H. Frank Heath, in "The Old English Alliterative Line," *Transactions of the Philological Society* (1894), 375–95, but see also Bernard ten Brink, *Early English Literature,* trans. Horace M. Kennedy (New York: Henry Holt, 1883). For Trautman, see "Die neueste Beowulfausgabe und die altenglische Verslehre,"

Bonner Beiträge zur Anglistik, 17 (1905), 175–91. See also Kaluza, pp. 70–71, for full table of examples. Others will be cited below.

12 Pope recognized this fact in the preface to his 1966 edition, p. xvi: "My statement on page 18 that rests, as employed by Leonard, were a device unknown to Kaluza is entirely untrue, though it seems to be true that Leonard rediscovered them, as it were, and used them at points where Kaluza did not."

13 Kaluza, pp. 71 and 75. All of this may seem to take Kaluza out of the school of equal timers. It does not only because his chief aim was to show how "various speech material" (as found in Sievers' types) might be "regulated . . . into verses of four members," that is, harmonized with the four-beat theory.

14 John Morris, "Sidney Lanier and Anglo-Saxon Verse Technic," *American Journal of Philology,* 20 (1899), 435–38.

15 Edwin B. Setzler, *On Anglo-Saxon Versification from the Standpoint of Modern English Versification,* University of Virginia Studies in Teutonic Languages, 5 (Baltimore: J. H. Furst, 1904), 7 and 14. Italics in the text are mine.

16 James Routh, "Anglo-Saxon Meter," *Modern Philology,* 21 (1923), 429–34. During these same years, of course, Sievers himself was retracting the rhythmical implications of his original theory and evolving one introducing specific temporal relations but based on his elusive *Schallanalyse* which he outlined in "Zu Cynewulf," *Neusprachliche Studien: Festgabe für Karl Luick,* (*Die neueren Sprachen,* 6 Beiheft, 1925), 60–81.

17 W. E. Leonard, "*Beowulf* and the Niebelungen Couplet," *University of Wisconsin Studies in Language and Literature,* 2 (1918), 123 and 132. Leonard translates: "The good-old-much-despised-and-often-pronounced-dead-but-on-this-account-only-so-much-the-more-tenaciously-clinging-to-life-Lach-mannian-four-accent theory."

18 "Four Footnotes to Papers on Germanic Metrics," *Studies in English Philology, A Miscellany in Honor of Frederick Klaeber* (Minneapolis: Univ. of Minnesota Press, 1929), p. 5.

19 Examples are from Pope, p. 164.

20 The "counter-proposals" will be taken up in the next section of this chapter.

21 Bede, "De Arte Metrica," *The Complete Works of Venerable Bede in the Original Latin,* ed. J. A. Giles (London: Whittaker, 1843), 6, 77. (Composed not by ratio of measures but by number of syllables examined at the judgment of the ears.)

22 "A New Approach to the Rhythm of *Beowulf,*" *PMLA,* 81 (1966), pp. 23–33. See also Robert D. Stevick, *Suprasegmentals, Meter, and the Manuscript of Beowulf* (The Hague: Mouton, 1968). A proposal that proceeds from Creed's work is that by Constance B. Hieatt, "A New Theory of Triple Rhythm in the Hypermetric Lines of Old English Verse," *Modern Philology,* 67 (1969), 1–8.

23 Eduard Sievers, *Altgermanische Metrik.* An abridged version appeared in H.

Paul's *Grundriss der germanischen Philologie,* II, 2 (Strasbourg, 1905), pp. 1–38. The major portion of the latter article has now been made available in an English translation by Gawaina D. Luster for *Essential Articles: Old English Poetry,* ed. Jess B. Bessinger, Jr., and Stanley J. Kahrl (Hamden, Conn.: Archon Books, 1968), pp. 267–88. For the sake of those readers who may not read German easily, my quotations will be from this translation.

24 Sievers, "Metrische Studien IV. Die altschwedischen Upplandslagh nebst Proben formverwandter germanischer Sagdichtung." *Abhandlungen der K. sächsischen Gesellschaft der Wissenschaften,* Philol.-hist. Klasse, Vol. 35 (Leipzig, 1918), pp. 163 ff., and passim.

25 See note 16 above.

26 P. Fijn Van Draat, "The Cursus in Old English Poetry," *Anglia,* 38 (1914), 377–404.

27 W. W. Greg, "The Five Types in Anglo-Saxon Verse," *MLR,* 20 (1925), 12–17.

28 E. W. Scripture, "Die Grundgetsetze des altenglischen Stabreimvers," *Anglia,* 52 (1928), 69–75.

29 S. O. Andrew, *The Old English Alliterative Measure* (Croydon: H. R. Grubb, 1931), pp. 7–8.

30 "Lift Patterns in Old English Verse," *English Literary History,* 8 (1941), 74–80. The quotes used are from this article. See also, however, his discussion of versification in *Widsith,* ed. Kemp Malone, *Anglistica,* 13 (1962), and his article in *RES,* 19 (1943), 201–204.

31 "Old English Verse and English Speech Rhythm," *Transactions of the Philological Society* (1947), 56–72. Passages used are from pp. 59 and 62.

32 A. J. Bliss, *The Metre of Beowulf* (Oxford: Basil Blackwell, 1958).

33 *Journal of English and Germanic Philology,* 59 (1960), 139. Hereafter cited as *JEGP.*

34 Elinor D. Clemons, "A Metrical Analysis of the Old English Poem *Exodus,*" Diss. Texas, 1961.

35 "Bliss's Light Verses in the *Beowulf,*" *JEGP,* 66 (1967), 230–40.

36 "Rules for Syntax and Metrics in *Beowulf,*" *JEGP,* 69 (1970), 81–88.

37 I will be doing much more with this concept in chapter 4 as I demonstrate my own work. In my 1964 dissertation, and in the article which appeared in 1975, I made a tentative hypothesis (influenced by Kaluza) of how the four-member verse generates all the types and variations found in *Beowulf,* but I did not press the theory (in the dissertation) beyond grouping the pulses accordingly since my major interest was in demonstrating measures. Because my analysis falls precisely into this same position in the historical framework as Cable's, I will be making reference to my previous work throughout the rest of this chapter.

38 I find Cable's conclusion unconvincing from his premise or hypothesis, and I will demonstrate my reasons as well as a new conclusion following from my 1964 hypothesis in chapter 4 below. However, in spite of the flaw I see in Cable's hypothesis, I nevertheless credit him for providing me—in his careful

analysis of stress and his insistence on four-member verses—with the support and data I needed to extend my hypothesis into a theory and demonstration.

39   "Timers, Stressers, and Linguists" (see n. 1 above). See also Ewald Standop, "Metric Theory Gone Astray," *Language and Style,* 8 (1975), 60–77. Early critics were James Sledd, "Old English Prosody: A Demurrer," *College English,* 31 (1969), 71–74; W. K. Wimsatt, "The Rule and the Norm: Halle and Keyser on Chaucer's Meter," ibid., 31 (1970), 774–88, and Karl Magnuson and Frank G. Ryder, "The Study of English Prosody: An Alternative Proposal," ibid., pp. 789–820.

40   His book was followed by another article, "Parallels to the Melodic Formulas of *Beowulf,*" *Modern Philology,* 73 (1975), 1–14.

41   Some of the history of this patterning, as well as the review of work done by the structural linguists on prosodic features, may be found in my articles "Adapting the Psalm Tones to English," *Liturgical Arts Quarterly,* 34 (1965), 7–12, and "Some Linguistic Criteria in the Accommodation of the English Mass Text to Sung Recitative and Melody," *Caecilia,* 91 (1964), 48–62.

42   Univ. of Texas.

43   Joynes, p. 96. I choose this particular passage because it incorporates both a complete sentence and most of the Five Types.

44   (New York: Harper & Row). It was preceded by Samuel Jay Keyser, "Old English Prosody," *College English,* 30 (1969), 331–56, and "Old English Prosody: A Reply," ibid., 31 (1969), 74–80.

45   Paull Franklin Baum, "The Meter of *Beowulf,*" *Modern Philology,* 46 (1948–49), 73–91, 145–62; Josef Taglicht, "*Beowulf* and Old English Verse Rhythm," *Review of English Studies,* 12 (1961), 347; and R. B. LePage, "A Rhythmical Framework for the Five Types," *English and Germanic Studies,* 6 (1957), 92–103.

46   Baum's careful progression with sufficient examples through the four variations is both logical and convincing, and seems to me to be his finest contribution. Perhaps it is only because he found no scheme for symbolizing his ideas that his work seems not to have become part of the general OE prosodic vocabulary.

47   Pope, p. 45.

48   "Formal Aspects of the Meter of *Beowulf,*" Diss. Vanderbilt 1951.

49   *The Larger Rhetorical Patterns in Anglo-Saxon Poetry* (New York: Columbia Univ. Press, 1935).

50   William Thomson, *The Rhythm of Speech* (Glasgow: Maclehose, Jackson, 1923).

51   See Richard L. Crocker, "*Musica Rhythmica* and *Musica Metrica* in Antique and Medieval Theory," *Journal of Music Theory,* 2 (1958), 2–23.

52   See Baum and Taglicht, as well as Bliss, who in making an analogy said of Gregorian Chant: "Its rhythm is variable, and is entirely dependent on the natural prose rhythm of the words sung; any such arbitrary lengthening of words and syllables as is required by the chronometric theory is quite alien to its nature" (pp. 107–108).

53   Peter Clemoes, *Liturgical Influence on Punctuation in Late Old English and Early Middle English Manuscripts,* Occasional Papers, No. 1 (Cambridge: Dept. of Anglo-Saxon, 1952).

54   See also Calvin S. Brown, "Can Musical Notation Help English Scansion?" *Journal of Aesthetics and Art Criticism,* 23 (1965), 329–34. Although his approach to the question is different from the one I suggest here, I agree with his conclusion that "as a normal method of scansion in English verse, musical notation indicates a regularity that I do not hear, creates more problems than it solves, and is in general more of a nuisance than a help" (p. 333).

CHAPTER 2

1   It must be emphasized that my use of Gregorian Chant as a means for studying the measurement of irregular rhythm is meant in no way to suggest that Gregorian Chant influenced the form of OE poetry. Such a suggestion would be preposterous since the Germanic meter is centuries older than Gregorian Chant. On the other hand, it would be possible although extraneous to this study to suggest the converse: That the irregular rhythms of the native poetry of the new European peoples stimulated the development of Gregorian Chant. See, for example, Willi Apel, *Gregorian Chant* (Bloomington: Indiana Univ. Press, 1958), p. 79: "As for the early sources of the standard repertory . . . it has often been noticed, though only grudgingly admitted, that none of them was written in Rome or, for that matter, in Italy. They all come from . . . the Franco-German empire. . . . What we call 'Gregorian Chant' represents an eighth-to-ninth century fusion of Roman and Frankish elements."

2   Curt Sachs, *Rhythm and Tempo: A Study in Music History* (New York: Norton, 1953), p. 247.

3   Again, if there is any suggestion of influence, it would be in the direction of the secular poetry influencing the development of Gregorian Chant, as noted also by J. Smits van Waesberghe, *Gregorian Chant and Its Place in the Catholic Liturgy* (Stockholm: Continental Book Company, n.d.), p. 47: "The immediate success of prose and sequence in the ninth century is . . . undoubtedly to be attributed to their relationship with the secular song, folksong. Despite their monastic segregation the monks remained men, who, with all their respect for the sacred liturgical plain chant, also knew the joy of giving expression to their feelings in songs of their own time: the tropes, sequences and proses are to be regarded as the religious folksongs of the monks and canons of the Middle Ages."

4   Introit for Pentecost Sunday, *Graduale Romanum* (Paris, Tournai, Rome: Desclée & Socii, 1948), p. 292.

5   My transcription follows that provided by van Waesberghe, p. 32, but with several changes in rhythmic interpretation.

6   Paull Franklin Baum, "The Meter of *Beowulf,*" *Modern Philology,* 46 (1948–49), p. 75.

7 See particularly Dom Dominic Johner, *A New School of Gregorian Chant,* 3rd English ed. by Herman Erpf and Max Ferrars (New York: Frederick Pustet, 1925).

8 See below for references to specific works containing the Solesmes theory.

9 There is no one clear presentation of this theory, but see, for example, J. W. A. Vollaerts, S.J., *Rhythmic Proportions in Early Medieval Ecclesiastical Chant* (Leiden: E. J. Brill, 1958).

10 Gustave Reese, in *Music in the Middle Ages with an Introduction on the Music of Ancient Times* (New York: Norton, 1940), p. 146, comments that for practical purposes "the versions of the Solesmes scholars have at least the advantages of agreeing with one another in method, which the transcriptions of the mensuralists do not." Furthermore, the Solesmes theory in the abstract applies either to pure melody or to language, as we shall see below.

11 For additional publication data not provided in the text, see the Selected Bibliography.

12 *Voices and Instruments in Christian Worship,* (Collegeville, Minn.: Liturgical Press, 1964).

13 Mocquereau, *Le Nombre musical grégorien,* Vol. 1, Part 1, trans. Aileen Tone (Tournai: Desclée, 1932), 49.

14 My use of the terms *boundary* and *break* comes from a combination of such sources as Ilse Lehiste, *Suprasegmentals* (Cambridge, Mass.: MIT Press, 1970), p. 147 and passim; Ernst Pulgram, *Syllable, Word, Nexus, Cursus* (The Hague: Mouton, 1970), especially pp. 30 and 117; Larry M. Hyman, *Phonology: Theory and Analysis* (New York: Holt, Rinehart and Winston, 1975), p. 194; Philip Lieberman, *Intonation, Perception, and Language,* Research Monograph No. 38 (Cambridge, Mass.: MIT Press, 1967), p. 110, and Noam Chomsky and Morris Halle, *The Sound Pattern of English* (New York: Harper & Row, 1968).

15 Citations from the *Beowulf* in this chapter are from Frederick Klaeber, *Beowulf and the Fight at Finnsburg,* 3rd ed. (Boston: Heath, 1950).

16 Lehiste says, "Suprasegmental features characteristically constitute patterns in time; the domain over which these patterns are manifested are phonological units of varying size (i.e. varying temporal extent)," p. 154. Further, "There is no question about the rhythmic structure of speech, and it seems reasonable to assume that rhythm is of fundamental importance in the neural organization of performance," p. 155.

17 Dom Joseph Gajard, *The Rhythm of Plainsong,* trans. Dom Aldhelm Dean (New York: J. Fisher, 1945), p. 18.

18 Lehiste says, pp. 119–20: "Stress perception . . . seems to be quite different from the perception of loudness. . . . It would perhaps be advisable to use the term *stress* to refer to prominence produced by means of respiratory effort (the 'expiratory accent' of older phoneticians), and to employ the term *accent* when prominence is achieved by other phonetic means in place of or in addition to respiratory effort. I shall continue to use the term *stress* to refer to linguistically significant prominence; however, I shall make clear in

instances where it is relevant which of the phonetic factors is involved in producing this prominence."

19 The full passage reads: "What has to be decided first is the minimum size of the unit of stress placement. From what is known of the activity of intercostal musculature, it appears probable that the smallest unit that may carry stress must be approximately the size of a syllable. The muscular gesture that underlies stress production requires a certain time for its realization, and there are time delays in the system that make it extremely unlikely that stress can be 'turned on' to coincide with the duration of a single segmental sound," p. 147.

20 David Abercrombie, "A Phonetician's View of Verse Structure," *Linguistics,* 6 (1964), pp. 5–6, describes the phenomenon as follows: "Each muscular contraction, and consequent rise in air-pressure, is a *chest-pulse* . . . and each chest-pulse constitutes a syllable. . . . There is in addition a second system of pulse-like muscular movements . . . [it] consists of a series of less frequent, more powerful contractions of the breathing muscles which every now and then coincide with, and reinforce, a chest pulse, and cause a more considerable and more sudden rise in air-pressure. These reinforcing movements constitute the system of *stress-pulses,* and this system is combined in speech with the system of chest pulses."

21 *A Course in Phonetics* (New York: Harcourt Brace Jovanovich, 1975).

22 Marie Pierik, *The Song of the Church* (New York: Longmans, Green, 1947), p. 190, says of anacrusis: "From the time of the German classic philologist Hermann (d. 1848) the *arsis* which precedes the first *thesis* of the melodic movement has been called *anacrusis.* In modern music the measure always starts on the down, or *thetic,* beat even though the *rhythm* may start with the up, or arsic element. As a matter of fact, 'there is no melody which starts with the heavy beat,' according to Riemann, and d'indy supplements this with the assertion that 'all melody starts with an anacrusis *expressed or understood*'." Mocquereau said it perhaps more succinctly, but in French: "Si l'on a bien compris la nature du rythme, c'est-à-dire l'union intime, indissoluble de l'arsis et de la thésis, on a compris du même coup combien inutile et dangereuse est la notion de l'anacrouse, telle que l'ont proposée, il y a un siècle environ, certains métriciens," *Nombre,* Part 3 (Tournai: Desclée, 1927), 663.

23 *The Rhythmic Structure of Music* (Chicago: Univ. of Chicago Press, 1960), p. 2.

24 See the first use of this example, pp. 32–33.

25 The Solesmes interpretation of the psalm tones, however, often recognized both the duration feature of classical Latin and the tonic feature of the vulgar or spoken Latin of the early Church. It did this by placing an ictus in the melodic line in a different position from where it would occur in the Latin text, or by dotting the punctum over a long vowel which occurs after the one taking the melodic ictus. For further discussion of this matter, see my article "Adapting the Psalm Tones to English," *Liturgical Arts Quarterly,* 34 (1965), 7–12.

26 Lehiste makes the distinction as follows: "When stress functions at the sentence level, it does not change the meaning of any lexical item, but it increases the relative prominence of the lexical items." She cites M. Bierwisch, "Regeln für die Intonation deutscher Sätze," *Studia Grammatica,* 7 (1966), 99–201, in distinguishing three kinds of sentence-level stress: a primary stress ("nonemphatic sentence stress"), contrastive stress, and emphatic stress (p. 150–51). In regard to emphatic stress, Ewald Standop, "Metric Theory Gone Astray: A Critique of the Halle-Keyser Theory," *Language and Style,* 8 (1975), says: "It is a well-known fact that practically any word can receive primary stress under suitable conditions" (p. 67).

CHAPTER 3

1 Cable, as we saw in chapter 1, reasserts in his book the principle of four-member verses in OE poetry. Although I made a similar hypothesis previously, I credit Cable with supplying the kind of evidence I needed to work my theory through as I do now.

2 My verse and line citations from *Beowulf* in chapters 3, 4, and 5 follow Klaeber, *Beowulf and the Fight at Finnsburg,* 3rd ed. (Boston: Heath, 1950) except where more of a line has been recovered since Klaeber's last edition. In these cases I follow C. L. Wrenn, *Beowulf With the Finnesburg Fragment* (London: George G. Harrap, 1958). However, in either case I transcribe the words within the verse directly from the manuscript facsimiles with an attempt to reproduce the spacing of the scribes whenever that is significant, except that I spell out abbreviations—other than 7 (ond)—and use "w" instead of the wen. Citations are based on the following facsimile editions: Kemp Malone, ed., *The Nowell Codex,* Early English Manuscripts in Facsimile, 12 (Copenhagen: Rosenkilde & Bagger, 1963); and Julius Zupitza, *Beowulf Reproduced in Facsimile from the Unique Manuscript,* 2nd ed. by Norman Davis, Early English Text Society, Original Ser., No. 245 (London: Oxford Univ. Press, 1959).

   Briefly, the spacing choices have been reduced to ½, 1, 1½, or 2 minims. The effect of these choices is always relative and occasionally indiscriminate. Since the amount of space between words and/or syllables in the *Beowulf* MS is relative (see n. 9 below) the mechanical spacing of fixed type will appear in one example disproportionate to that in another and in relation to the variance in the MS facsimile. Space between morphs in the printed representation here must be read as relative to other spacing within the single line or passage only. Hence, the fact that there is, or is no, spacing between certain morphs, and that there is twice as much between others, is the only information that can be registered in some instances; the visual effect does not duplicate the facsimile. And doubtless the exigencies of modern publishing renders some instances as clear misreadings of the scribes handiwork.

3 Morris Halle and Samuel Jay Keyser, *English Stress* (New York: Harper & Row, 1971), treat this under three headings: stress weakening (p. 15),

compound rule (p. 19 ff.), and alternating stress rule (p. 27). See also Noam
Chomsky and Halle, *The Sound Pattern of English* (New York: Harper &
Row, 1968), p. 50, and Larry M. Hyman, *Phonology: Theory and Analysis*
(New York: Holt, Rinehart and Winston, 1975), p. 201.

4 I accept the presence of intermediate stress in types D and E as part of the
metrical pattern, as demonstrated in Cable, *MM,* especially chapter 4.

5 Cf. Peter Ladefoged, *A Course in Phonetics* (New York: Harcourt Brace
Jovanovich, 1975), p. 160: "In the case of voiced sounds, the vibrating vocal
cords chop up the stream of lung air so that pulses of relatively high pressure
alternate with moments of lower pressure."

6 For the purposes of my study I accept the syllable as a sound element and do
not find it necessary to review the linguistic definitions, since, as Ladefoged
says, "Although nearly everybody can identify syllables, almost nobody can
define them" (*op. cit.,* p. 218). Cf. also Hyman, *Phonology:* "Unlike the
phoneme, which represents an abstract distinctive unit of sound which is part
of the speaker's knowledge of his language, the syllable may simply be a unit
required for the production or perception of utterance" (p. 194).

7 See also Baum, who says that "as far as meter or scansion is concerned, it
does not appear that he [the poet] regarded syllabic length as functional" (pp.
158–59). Keyser in his 1969 article, "Old English Prosody," *College English*
30, ruled out a metrical significance to long and short syllables (p. 349), on
the basis that a distinction would render too many of the lines in *Beowulf*
unmetrical.

8 Even Pope, whose system rests on the principle of isochronous timing, does
not assign a consistently longer duration to long syllables than to short ones.
For example, see in his first ten lines of *Beowulf,* p. 164, line 7, how three of
the long vowels take an eighth note while one inflected ending, -en of *funden,*
takes a quarter note. Or see any other lines in his selection.

9 I find the spacing very closely related to the environment, which would make
it impossible to measure by instrument according to any one system of
classification. In the work of both scribes we find both very compact sections
where letters are noticeably linked together or spaced apart and other
sections where there is an overall looseness which makes the same amount of
space used in other sections meaningless in these.

For attempts at somewhat systematic interpretations of the manuscript
spacings, see especially Robert D. Stevick, *Suprasegmentals, Meter, and the
Manuscript of Beowulf* (The Hague: Mouton, 1968), who gives special attention to morphic spacing; Joynes, pp. 69–72, who says, "The fact that the
scribes were writing something which they actually heard in the linguistic and
poetic system seems evident, both on the basis of the consistency of the
spacing in both hands and the correspondences between these spaces and
observed metrical and syntactic structures" (p. 72); and John A. Nist,
"Textual Elements in the *Beowulf* Manuscript," *Papers of the Michigan
Academy of Science, Arts, and Letters,* 42 (1957), 331–38. The essay is also
included in Nist, *The Structure and Texture of Beowulf.* Nist says, "When the

Beowulf scribes, therefore, write contiguous stressed morphemes as separate elements and make stressless morphemes adhere to stressed morphemes, they are using a most efficient method of indicating the realities of Old English linguistic structure on its suprasegmental plane" (p. 338). Already in 1921 Margarete Rademacher suggested in her Münster dissertation, *Die Worttrennung in angel-sächsischen Handschriften,* that the spacings were a result of unconscious "self-dictation."

10   *The Phoneme: Its Nature and Use,* 2nd ed. (Cambridge: W. Heffer, 1962), p. 70.

11   Randolph Quirk and C. L. Wrenn, *An Old English Grammar,* 2nd ed. (London: Methuen, 1958), p. 14.

12   Touster, p. 126.

13   My practice of scanning what the tenth century scribe recorded, rather than accepting as accurate only what the original meter may have allowed in rhythmical variations, echoes the view expressed by W. P. Lehmann and Takemitzu Tabusa, *The Alliterations of the Beowulf* (Austin: Univ. of Texas, 1958), who found it "more realistic, and of greater importance for critical analysis, to recognize that the changing language forced changing patterns on the Old English poets, modifications of the patterns they had learned as a part of their craft" (p. 8).

14   See Joynes, "Structural Analysis," pp. 30–35. Perhaps I should add here that my midwest plains background makes all of this sound perfectly reasonable to me, whereas someone from, say, New England, may not be able to accept it. In this connection I always remember being corrected by a New England confrere for pronouncing "known" as [no + ən] or [no + wən], whereas the "correct" pronunciation was [no:n].

15   However, I never use manuscript markings as the primary support for a prosodic interpretation, but only as additional support when other evidence has already fairly well settled the matter under consideration. Nevertheless, I include a statistical presentation of the points and accents as an appendix to this study.

16   Elliott Van Kirk Dobbie, *Beowulf and Judith, The Anglo-Saxon Poetic Records,* 4 (New York: Columbia Univ. Press, 1953), xxx, says that it is impossible to be certain of the number. Zupitza has some 670. Malone added some eighteen as a result of his reading of the Thorkelin transcripts (see *PMLA,* 64 [1949], 1190–1218). But scholars differ widely in using specific numbers: Nist makes it 889, Joynes, 666.

17   How stress operates in meter is also discussed in two articles that I found useful: Paul Kiparsky, "Stress, Syntax, and Meter," *Language,* 51 (1975), 576–616; and G. Knowles, "The Rhythm of English Syllables," *Lingua,* 34 (1974), 115–47.

18   Alternate readings of lines of this type, of course, change statistics, since some readings give the line an additional measure, which would put it in a different grouping here. Whether or not the separate measure in a line break should be counted (since in a few eight-measure long lines it makes a ninth)

is another question that affects statistics. Hence, my figures should be read as approximations only.

19 Cf. Cable, *MM* 25–27.

20 The thirteen verses are the following: a-verses 301 and 1767; b-verses 257, 441, 641, 950, 996, 1168, 1238, 1353, 1625, 2801, and 3057.

21 The five are all a-verses: 234, 1425, 1545, 1732, 1758.

CHAPTER 4

1 We sometimes encounter this same situation in the purely melodic patterns of the Gregorian Chant. For example, in the Alleluia verse of Pentecost Sunday we have this pattern surrounding a half bar: ♪♪♪♪ . This would ordinarily count 123 123 | 12, but cannot because the bar requires a count too. Hence, the Solesmes school dots the final punctum before the bar (the second note of a podatus) in order to give it the metrical ictus necessary to take care of the bar. It counts then as 123 12 123 12 and would appear thus: ♪♪♪♪ (*Graduale Romanum,* p. 293, and van Waesberghe, p. 34).

2 It may be noted in connection with these readings, that Pope's third and fourth degrees of stress usually coincide with my placement of the ictus in such cases as these. Thus I find Pope's sense of rhythm, as such, more trustworthy than Bliss's, for example, once I have separated his markings from the two isochronous measures he forces them to fill. The similarity of my use of the preceding line break in this type of verse to Pope's "initial rest" is too obvious for further comment, except that, again, I admit no question of filling isochronous measures.

3 John Nist, "Textual Elements in the *Beowulf* Manuscript," *Papers of the Michigan Academy of Science, Arts, and Letters,* 42 (1957), 337.

4 Cable says something of the same, perhaps in reverse, *MM* 77–78.

5 Cable, *MM* 29, says the pattern could occur but does not. I think we have evidence that it does.

CHAPTER 5

1 Klaeber and Wrenn retain 947a, 187b, 3124a, but emend 1546a, 1889a, 2673a, and 1404b.

2 A question is raised concerning the alliteration, and I will say more about this below. But see also Paull Franklin Baum, "The Meter of *Beowulf*," *Modern Philology,* 46 (1949), 151: "Double alliteration in the second verse is rare, but it is well attested." He cites 574, 1772, etc.

3 Cf. Richard A. Lewis, "Alliteration and Old English Metre," *Medium Ævum,* 42 (1973), 119–31.

4 Cf. Constance, B. Hieatt, "Alliterative Patterns in the Hypermetric Lines of Old English Verse," *Modern Philology,* 71 (1973), 237–42.

5 Perhaps *æt* alliterates with *æl:* xx x́+ x́ x | xxx x́+ x́ x .

6   D. G. Scragg's article, "Initial *H* in Old English," *Anglia,* 88 (1970), 165–96
    (although I discovered it after I had originally proposed this hypothesis),
    supplies the kind of evidence I needed for support.
7   The other lines emending *hunferð* are 1488, 1165. The other lines emending
    hond are 2094, 1541, 2972.
8   It seems to me that Lewis's article explores this question.

APPENDIX

1   The additional markings used with the points at the end of sections can for
    our purposes be considered in the same category as simple points; the two
    colon-like marks we discussed in chapter 5.
2   Elliott Van Kirk Dobbie, *Beowulf and Judith, The Anglo-Saxon Poetic
    Records,* 4 (New York: Columbia Univ. Press, 1953), xxx, says that it is
    impossible to be certain of the number. Zupitza has some 670. Malone added
    some eighteen as a result of his reading of the Thorkelin transcripts (see
    PMLA, 64 (1949), 1190–1218). But scholars differ widely in using specific
    numbers: Nist makes it 889, Joynes, 666.
3   Joynes, p. 80, says, "In linguistic terms, therefore, the Punctum represents the
    sustained vowel quality which accompanies a terminal juncture and falls on
    the last vowel in the juncture morpheme or on an entire monotone mor-
    pheme." This seems correct in structural terms, but the awkward definition
    she gives for the chant punctum, and on which she bases her statement, is
    inaccurate. For the punctum in the chant, the $\equiv\blacksquare\equiv$, does not represent
    lengthening. It represents the *prótos chrónos*, which may be the shortest
    syllable in the language, and originally it may have meant a lower pitch (see
    Mocquereau, *Nombre,* II, 146). A "dot" with a punctum (in modern editions
    of chant), on the other hand, does represent lengthening, and had some
    origins in the early manuscripts, but not as a square note, and it should not be
    confused with the actual punctum. It is the dotted punctum that "usually
    appears at the end of major phrases and before the 'breath marks' at the end
    of such phrases" (p. 79). Nist, "Textual Elements," p. 332, says, "Examination
    of all occurrences of the period proves that it is a rhythmic-unit marker
    having little or no connection with those tone changes or pause values
    reflected in the punctuation of Modern English."
4   I found after my analysis that my conclusions are in substantial agreement
    with those demonstrated by Joynes. Since she gave individual treatment to
    each of the thirteen lines, I will not repeat here an analysis of lines about
    which there is no question.
5   Nist, "Textual Elements," pp. 334–37.
6   Joynes, p. 80. G. C. Thornley, on the other hand, in "The Accents and Points
    of MS. Junius 11," *Transactions of the Philological Society* (London, 1954),
    178–205, interprets the accents in the Junius 11 manuscript as providing the
    indications for intonations and inflections in a liturgical recitative. Although
    I think his interpretation rests on too few consistently applicable accent

situations, I find this statement credible: "We must assume that all the accents were inserted to assist a lector probably in a monastery" (p. 182).

7 Others in this category of "phrase stress before | " are, of type B: 442b, 507a, 660b, 821a, 1147b, 1201b, 1274b, 1297a, 1313b, 1863b, 1960b, 2002a, 2084a, 2103b, 2147b, 2258b, 2287a, 2308b, 2553b, 3164b, 2568b, 2577b, 2679b, 2736b, 2769b, 2898b, 2944b, 2992b, 3116b, 3123b. Type E: 123b, 603b, 759b, 911a, 1187a, 1720b, 1870b, 1965b, 2302b, 2543a, 2559b, 2584b, 2820b, 3119a. Type C: 386b(2), 1116b. As in the example, so in these two Cs also, the accents are on words that have been "de-contracted" by modern editors. Line 386b will be discussed among the anomalous verses because of the other of the two accent marks found over it.

8 Others in the category "phrase stress + phrase stress" are, of type D: 742a, 1307a, 1407b, and 128b (which Bliss indexes as E: I suggest the accent supports Sievers' and Pope's D reading). Type C: 544b, 975b, 1167a, 1233a, 1331b, 1685b, 2263b, 2858a, 1149a, 1445a, 1850a, 2346a, 2514b, 2641a, 3010a.

9 Others in the category "phrase stress + secondary stress" are, of type E: 895b, 1882b, 1924b, 2080b. (Of these, 2080b: *lic èall for swéalg,* might deserve some reexamination, since the accent over *lic* could well support a primary accent on *eall,* thus making it a D type, removing it then from this category to the previous one of juxtaposed primary stresses.) Type D: 1895a, 1962a, 2674a, 2689a. And type A: 690a, 780a, 1652a, 3147a(1), 1516a, 2607a.

10 On the other hand, in the type B verse (537a) the accent does coincide with Sievers' placement of the caesura in all B type verses. Perhaps this takes the verse out of this category and places it in the next one, thereby further emphasizing the reduction of the secondary stress.

11 The others in the category "phrase + weak" that follow the typical examples are, of type A: 300b, 1162a, 1163a (a hypermetric verse), 1177b, 1223b, 1394b, 1492a, 1562a, 1863a, 2086a, 2270a, 2666a, 2681a, 2743a, 2751a, 3025a, 3138a. Of type B: 579b, 1121b, 1528b, 1587b, 2210b, 2230b, 2280b, 2468b, 2701b.

12 Others in the category "secondary before | " are, of type A: 2109a, 2258a, 2342a, 2376a, 2661a, 3147a(2). Of type D: 1038a, 1966a, 2558a, 2964a, 3063a.

13 The other three are 2155b, 2631a, and 3076a.

14 Lehmann and Tabusa, *Alliterations,* say that "verbs standing first in the line would by archaic practices have had predominant accent" (p. 6), and the article by Willard and Clemons reviewed precisely those verses with verbs in initial positions. Cable supports this position also.

15 Nist, "Textual Elements," p. 336.

A SELECTED BIBLIOGRAPHY

OLD ENGLISH TEXTS AND STUDIES

Anderson, L. F. *The Anglo-Saxon Scop.* Univ. of Toronto Studies, Philological Series I. Toronto: Univ. Librarian, 1903.

Andrew, Samuel Ogden. *The Old English Alliterative Measure.* Croydon: H. R. Grubb, 1931.

———. *Postscript on Beowulf.* Cambridge: Cambridge Univ. Press, 1948.

Bartlett, Adeline C. *The Larger Rhetorical Patterns in Anglo-Saxon Poetry.* New York: Columbia Univ. Press, 1935.

Bauer, Gerd. "The Problem of Short Diphthongs in Old English." *Anglia,* 74 (1956), 427–37.

Baum, Paull Franklin. "The Meter of *Beowulf.*" *MP,* 46 (1948–49), 73–91, 145–62.

Bessinger, J. B. "Oral to Written: Some Implications of the Anglo-Saxon Transition." *Explorations,* 8 (1957), 11–15.

Bliss, A. J. *The Metre of Beowulf.* 2nd ed. rev., 1958. Oxford: Basil Blackwell, 1967.

Cable, Thomas M. "Rules for Syntax and Metrics in *Beowulf.*" *JEGP,* 69 (1970), 81–88.

———. "Timers, Stressers, and Linguists: Contention and Compromise." *MLQ,* 33 (1972), 227–39.

———. *The Meter and Melody of Beowulf.* Urbana: Univ. of Illinois Press, 1974.

———. "Parallels to the Melodic Formulas of *Beowulf.*" *MP,* 73 (1975), 1–14.

Clemoes, Peter. *Liturgical Influence on Punctuation in Late Old English and Early Middle English Manuscripts.* Occasional Papers I. Cambridge: Dept. of Anglo-Saxon, 1952.

Clemons, Elinor Diederich. "A Metrical Analysis of the Old English Poem *Exodus.*" Diss. Texas, 1961.

Clemons-Kyte, Elinor Diederich. "On the Composition of Hypermetric Verses in Old English." *MP,* 71 (1973), 160–65.

Creed, Robert P. "A New Approach to the Rhythm of *Beowulf.*" *PMLA,* 81 (1966), 23–33.

Daunt, Marjorie. "Old English Sound Changes Reconsidered in Relation to Scribal Tradition and Practice." *Transactions of the Philological Society* (1939), 108–37.

———. "Old English Verse and English Speech Rhythm." *Transactions of the Philological Society* (1947), 56–72.

Dobbie, Elliott Van Kirk. *Beowulf and Judith.* The Anglo-Saxon Poetic Records, vol. 4. New York: Columbia Univ. Press, 1953.

Greg. W. W. "The Five-Types in Anglo-Saxon Verse." *MLR,* 20 (1925), 12–17.

Heath, H. Frank. "The Old English Alliterative Line." *Transactions of the Philological Society* (1894), 375–95.

Heusler, Andreas. *Deutsche Versgeschichte, mit Einschluss des altenglischen und altnordischen Stabreimverses,* I and II, *Gundriss der germanischen Philologie,* 8. Berlin and Leipzig: Walter de Gruyter, 1925.

Hieatt, Constance B. "A New Theory of Triple Rhythm in the Hypermetric Lines of Old English Verse." *MP,* 67 (1969), 1–8.

———. "Alliterative Patterns in the Hypermetric Lines of Old English Verse." *MP,* 71 (1973), 237–42.

Joynes, Mary Lu. "Structural Analysis of Old English Metrics." Diss. Texas, 1958.

Kaluza, Max. *A Short History of English Versification from the Earliest Times to the Present Day.* Trans. A. C. Dunston. London: George Allen, 1911.

Keyser, Samuel Jay. "Old English Prosody." *CE,* 30 (1969), 331–56.

Keyser, Samuel Jay, and Halle, Morris. "Old English Alliterative Meter." *English Stress: Its Form, Its Growth, and Its Role in Verse.* New York: Harper & Row, 1971, pp. 147–64.

Klaeber, Frederick. *Beowulf and the Fight at Finnsburg.* 3rd ed. Boston: Heath, 1950.

Kuhn, Sherman M. "The Old English Digraph: A Reply." *Language,* 31 (1955), 390–401.

Kuhn, Sherman M., and Quirk, Randolph. "Some Recent Interpretations of Old English Digraph Spellings." *Language,* 29 (1953), 143–56.

Lehmann, Winifred P. *The Development of Germanic Verse Form.* Austin: Univ. of Texas Press, 1956.

———. "Metrical Evidence for Old English Suprasegmentals." *TSLL,* 1 (1959), 66–72.

Lehmann, Winifred P., and Takemitsu Tabusa. *The Alliterations of the Beowulf.* Austin: Univ. of Texas Press, 1958.

Leonard, William Ellery. "*Beowulf* and the Niebelungen Couplet." *University of Wisconsin Studies in Language and Literature,* 2 (1918), 99–152.

———. "Four Footnotes to Papers on Germanic Metrics." *Studies in English Philology: A Miscellany in Honor of Frederick Klaeber.* Ed. Kemp Malone and Martin B. Rund. Minneapolis: Univ. of Minnesota Press, 1929, pp. 1–13.

LePage, R. B. "A Rhythmical Framework for the Five Types." *English and Germanic Studies,* 6 (1957), 92–103.

Lewis, Richard A. "Alliteration and Old English Metre." *Medium Ævum,* 42 (1973), 119–30.

Luecke, Jane Marie. "Meter and the Free Rhythm of Beowulf." Diss. Notre Dame, 1964.

———. Review of *Suprasegmentals, Meter, and the Manuscript of Beowulf* by Robert D. Stevick. *Linguistics,* 62 (1970), 110–17.

———. "Measuring the Rhythmic Variations of Old English Meter." *Language and Style,* 8 (1975), 95–110.

Malone, Kemp. "Lift Patterns in Old English Verse." *ELH,* 8 (1941), 74–80.

———. "Pluralinear Units in Old English Poetry." *RES,* 19 (1943), 201–204.

———. "Readings from the Thorkelin Transcripts of *Beowulf.*" *PMLA,* 64 (1949), 1190–1218.

———, ed. *Widsith. Anglistica,* 13 (1962).

———, ed. *The Nowell Codex: British Museum Cotton Vitellius A, XV Second MS,* Early English Manuscripts in Facsimile, 12. Copenhagen: Rosenkilde & Bagger, 1963.

Morris, John. "Sidney Lanier and Anglo-Saxon Verse Technic." *American Journal of Philology,* 20 (1899), 435–38.

Nist, John A. "Textual Elements in the *Beowulf* Manuscript." *Papers of the Michigan Academy of Science, Arts, and Letters,* 42 (1957), 331–38.

———. *The Structure and Texture of Beowulf.* São Paulo, Brazil: Univ. of São Paulo Press, 1959.

Pope, John Collins, *The Rhythm of Beowulf: An Interpretation of the Normal and Hypermetric Verse-Forms in Old English Poetry.* 2nd ed., New Haven: Yale Univ. Press, 1966.

Prokosch, Eduard. "Two Types of Scribal Errors in the *Beowulf* MS." *Studies in English Philology: A Miscellany in Honor of Frederick Klaeber.* Ed. Kemp Malone and Martin B. Rund. Minneapolis: Univ. of Minnesota Press, 1929, pp. 196–207.

Quirk, Randolph, and Wrenn, C. L. *An Old English Grammar.* 2nd ed. London: Methuen, 1958.

Reszkiewicz, Alfred. "The Phonemic Interpretation of Old English Digraphs." *Bulletin de la Société polonaise de linguistique,* 12 (Cracow, 1953), 179–87.

Routh, James. "Anglo-Saxon Meter." *MP,* 21 (1923), 429–34.

Samuels, M. L. "The Study of Old English Phonology." *Transactions of the Philological Society* (1953), 15–47.

Schipper, Jakob. *A History of English Versification.* Oxford: Clarendon Press, 1910.

Scragg, D. G. "Initial *H* in Old English." *Anglia,* 88 (1970), 165–96.

Scripture, E. W. "Die Grundgesetze des altenglischen Stabreimvers." *Anglia* 52 (1928), 69–75.

Setzler, Edwin B. *On Anglo-Saxon Versification from the Standpoint of Modern English Versification.* Univ. of Virginia Studies in Teutonic Languages, 5. Baltimore: J. H. Furst, 1904.

Sievers, Eduard. *Altgermanische Metrik.* Halle: M. Niemeyer, 1893.

———. "Zur Rhythmik des germanischen Alliterationsverses." *Paul and Braune's Beiträge,* 10 (1885), 209–314.

———. "Metrische Studien IV. Die altschwedischen Upplandslagh nebst Proben formverwandter germanischer Sagdichtung." *Abhandlungen der K. sächsischen Gesellschaft der Wissenschaften,* Philol.-hist. Klasse, Vol. 35. Leipzig, 1918, pp. 163 ff., and passim.

———. "Zu Cynewulf." *Neusprachliche Studien: Festgabe für Karl Luick. Die neueren Sprachen,* 6 (1925), 60–81.

Sisam, Kenneth. *Studies in the History of Old English Literature.* Oxford: Clarendon Press, 1953.

Slay, D. "Some Aspects of the Technique of Composition of Old English Verse." *Transactions of the Philological Society* (1952), 1–14.

Sledd, James. "Old English Prosody: A Demurrer." *CE,* 31 (1969), 71–74.

Smith, A. H. "The Photography of Manuscripts." *London Medieval Studies,* I, Part 2, Ed. R. W. Chambers, et al. Kendal: Titus Wilson & Sons, 1939.

Stevick, Robert D. *Suprasegmentals, Meter, and the Manuscript of Beowulf.* The Hague: Mouton, 1968.

Stockwell, Robert P. "The Phonology of Old English: A Structural Sketch." *Studies in Linguistics,* 13 (1958), 13–24.

Stockwell, Robert P., and C. W. Barritt. *Some Old English Graphemic-Phonemic Correspondences—æ, ea & A.* Washington, D. C., 1951.

Taglicht, Josef. "*Beowulf* and Old English Verse Rhythm." *RES,* 12 (1961), 341–51.

Ten Brink, Bernard. *Early English Literature.* Trans. Horace M. Kennedy. New York: Henry Holt, 1883.

Thornley, G. C. "The Accents and Points of MS Junius 11." *Transactions of the Philological Society* (1954), 178–205.

Touster, Eva Katherine. "Formal Aspects of the Meter of *Beowulf.*" Diss. Vanderbilt, 1951.

———. "Metrical Variation as a Poetic Device in *Beowulf.*" *Anglia,* 73 (1955), 115–26.

Trautmann, Moritz. "Die neueste Beowulfausgabe und die altenglische Verslehre." *Bonner Beiträge zur Anglistik,* 17 (1905), 175–91.

Van Draat, P. Fijn. "The Cursus in Old English Poetry." *Anglia,* 38 (1914), 377–404.

Watts, Ann Chalmers. *The Lyre and the Harp.* New Haven: Yale Univ. Press, 1969.

Wells, B. J. "Long Vowels and Diphthongs in Old Germanic and Old English." *Transactions of the American Philological Association,* 18 (1887), 134–57.

Willard, Rudolph, and Elinor D. Clemons. "Bliss's Light Verses in the *Beowulf.*" *JEGP,* 66 (1967), 230–40.

Wrenn, C. L. *Beowulf with the Finnesburg Fragment.* 2nd ed. rev. London: George G. Harrap, 1958.

———. "On the Continuity of English Poetry." *Anglia,* 76 (1958), 41–59.

———. "Two Anglo-Saxon Harps." *Studies in Old English in Honor of Arthur G. Brodeur.* Ed. Stanley B. Greenfield. Eugene: Univ. of Oregon Books, 1963.

Zupitza, Julius. *Beowulf.* Ed. Norman Davis. 2nd ed. Early English Text Society. Original Series, No. 245. London: Oxford Univ. Press, 1959.

STUDIES IN ENGLISH PROSODY AND LINGUISTICS

Abercrombie, David. "A Phonetician's View of Verse Structure." *Linguistics,* 6 (1964), 5–13.

―――. *Elements of General Phonetics.* Edinburgh: Edinburgh Univ. Press, 1967.

Baum, Paull Franklin. *The Other Harmony of Prose: An Essay in English Prose Rhythm.* Durham, N. C.: Duke Univ. Press, 1952.

Bolinger, Dwight. "Accent Is Predictable (If You're a Mind Reader)." *Language,* 48 (1972), 633–44.

Bowley, C. C. "Metrics and the Generative Approach." *Linguistics,* 121 (1974), 5–19.

Brown, Calvin S. "Can Musical Notation Help English Scansion?" *Journal of Aesthetics and Art Criticism,* 23 (1965), 329–34.

Chatman, Seymour B. *A Theory of Meter. Janua Linguarum* 36. The Hague: Mouton, 1965.

Chomsky, Noam, and Morris Halle, *The Sound Pattern of English.* New York: Harper & Row, 1968.

College English, 31 (May, 1970) and 33 (November, 1971). (Two issues devoted to theories of prosody.)

Collier, René. "Intonation from a Structural Linguistic Viewpoint: A Criticism." *Linguistics,* 129 (1974), 5–28.

Croll, Morris W. "Music and Metrics." *Studies in Philology,* 20 (1923), 388–94.

Crystal, David. *Prosodic Systems and Intonation in English.* Cambridge Studies in Linguistics, 1. Cambridge: Cambridge Univ. Press, 1969.

Crystal, David, and Randolph Quirk. *Systems of Prosodic and Paralinguistic Features in English.* The Hague: Mouton, 1964.

Drommel, R. "Ein Überblick über die bisherigen Arbeiten zur Sprechpause." *Phonetica,* 30 (1974), 221–38.

De Groot, A. W. "Phonetics in Its Relation to Aesthetics." *Manual of Phonetics.* Ed. L. Kaiser. Amsterdam: North-Holland Publishing Company, 1957, pp. 385–400.

Epstein, Edmund L., and Terrence Hawkes. *Linguistics and English Prosody. Studies in Linguistics,* Occasional Papers, 7. Buffalo, N. Y.: Univ. of Buffalo Press, 1959.

Forrest, William Craig. "Literary Kinesthesia: The Artistic Import of Sensuous Perception Concerned with the Articulatory Stratum of Literature in the Light of Recent Critical Theory and Poetic Practice." Diss. St. Louis Univ., 1960.

Frye, Northrop. "Lexis and Melos." *Sound and Poetry.* New York: Columbia Univ. Press, 1957.

Halle, Morris. "Stress Rules in English: A New Version." *Linguistic Inquiry,* 4 (1974), 451–64.

Halle, Morris, and Samuel Jay Keyser. "Chaucer and the Study of Prosody." *CE,* 28 (1966), 187–219.

―――. *English Stress: Its Form, Its Growth, and Its Role in Verse.* New York: Harper & Row, 1971.

Halpern, Martin. "On the Two Chief Metrical Modes in English." *PMLA,* 77 (1962), 177–86.

Hendern, Joseph W. "Time and Stress in English Verse." *Rice University Pamphlet,* 46 (1959).

Hendern, Joseph W., W. K. Wimsatt, Jr., and Monroe C. Beardsley. "A Word for Rhythm and a Word for Meter." *PMLA,* 76 (1961), 300–303.

Hollander, John. "The Music of Poetry." *Journal of Aesthetics and Art Criticism,* 15 (1956), 232–44.

Hyman, Larry M. *Phonology: Theory and Analysis.* New York: Holt, Rinehart and Winston, 1975.

Jeaffreson, J. W. "Stress and Rhythm in Speech." *Transactions of the Philological Society,* (1938), 73–95.

Jones, Daniel. *The Phoneme: Its Nature and Use.* 2nd ed. Cambridge: W. Heffer, 1962.

Kiparsky, Paul. "Stress, Syntax, and Meter." *Language,* 51 (1975), 576–616.

Knowles, G. "The Rhythm of English Syllables." *Lingua,* 34 (1974), 115–47.

Ladefoged, Peter. *Preliminaries to Linguistic Phonetics.* Chicago: Univ. of Chicago Press, 1971.

————. *A Course in Phonetics.* New York: Harcourt Brace Jovanovich, 1975.

La Drière, Craig. "Structure, Sound, and Meaning." *Sound and Poetry.* Ed. Northrop Frye. New York: Columbia Univ. Press, 1957, pp. 85–108.

————. "Prosody." *Dictionary of World Literature.* Ed. Joseph T. Shipley. Patterson, N. J.: Littlefield, Adams, 1960.

Lebedeva, N. V. "Certain Syntagmatic Features of Poetic Speech." *Linguistics,* 141 (1974), 35–42.

Lehiste, Ilse. *Suprasegmentals.* Cambridge, Mass.: MIT Press, 1970.

Levenston, E. A. "A Scheme for the Inter-relation of Linguistic Analysis and Poetry Criticism." *Linguistics,* 129 (1974), 29–47.

Lieberman, Philip. *Intonation, Perception, and Language.* Research Monograph No. 38. Cambridge, Mass.: MIT Press, 1967.

Lotman, Ju. M. "On Some Principle Difficulties in the Structural Description of a Text." *Linguistics,* 121 (1974), 57–63.

Lotz, John. "Metrics." *Current Trends in Linguistics.* Ed. Thomas A. Sebeok. Vol. 12. The Hague: Mouton, 1974, pp. 963–82.

Malof, Joseph: "The Native Rhythm of English Meters." *TSLL,* 5 (1964), 580–94.

Omond, Thomas Stewart. *English Metrists: Being a Sketch of English Prosodical Criticism from Elizabethan Times to the Present Day.* Oxford: Clarendon Press, 1921.

Patterson, William Morrison. *The Rhythm of Prose.* New York: Columbia Univ. Press, 1916.

Pike, Kenneth L. *The Intonation of American English.* Ann Arbor: Univ. of Michigan Press, 1946.

Pulgram, Ernst. *Syllable, Word, Nexus, Cursus.* The Hague: Mouton, 1970.

Saintsbury, George. *A History of English Prosody from the Twelfth Century to the Present Day.* London: Macmillan, 1906.

Shen, Yao, and Giles G. Peterson. *Isochronism in English.* Studies in Linguistics, Occasional Papers, 9. Buffalo, N. Y.: Univ. of Buffalo Press, 1962.

Smith, Henry Lee, Jr. "Toward Redefining English Prosody." *Studies in Linguistics,* 14 (1959), 68–75.

Snell, Ada L. F. *Pause: A Study of Its Nature and Its Rhythmical Function in Verse, Especially Blank Verse.* Ann Arbor: Univ. of Michigan Press, 1918.

Standop, Ewald. "Metric Theory Gone Astray." *Language and Style,* 8 (1975), 60–77.

Tarlinskaja, M. G. "Verse—Prose—Metre." *Linguistics,* 129 (1974), 63–86.

Thompson, John. *The Founding of English Metre.* New York: Columbia Univ. Press, 1961.

Thomson, William. *The Rhythm of Speech.* Glasgow: Maclehose, Jackson, 1923.

Trager, George L., and Henry Lee Smith, Jr. *An Outline of English Structure. Studies in Linguistics,* Occasional Papers, 3. Norman, Okla.: Battenburg Press, 1951.

Wimsatt, W. K., ed. *Versification: Major Language Types.* New York: MLA, 1972.

Wimsatt, W. K., and Monroe Beardsley. "The Concept of Meter: An Exercise in Abstraction." *PMLA,* 74 (1959), 585–98.

STUDIES IN RHYTHM, MUSIC, AND GREGORIAN CHANT

Alette, Carl. "Theories of Rhythm." 2 vols. Diss. Eastman School of Music, 1951.

Apel, Willi. *Gregorian Chant.* Bloomington: Indiana Univ. Press, 1966.

Angier, R. P. "The Aesthetics of Unequal Division." *Harvard Psychological Studies,* 1. Ed. Hugo Munsterberg. New York: Macmillan, 1903, pp. 541–61.

Augustine, St. "On Music" (*De Musica*). Trans. Robert Catesby Taliaferro. *The Fathers of the Church: Writings of St. Augustine,* II. Ed. Ludwig Schopp. New York: Fathers of the Church, 1947, pp. 151–379.

Beare, William. *Latin Verse and European Song: A Study in Accent and Rhythm.* London: Methuen, 1957.

———. "*Pollicis Ictus,* the Saturnian, and *Beowulf.*" *Classical Philology,* 50 (1955), 89–97.

Bede. "De Arte Metrica." *Complete Works of Venerable Bede in the Original Latin.* Ed. J. A. Giles. Vol. 6. London: Whittaker, 1843, pp. 40–79.

Bissell, Arthur D. *The Role of Expectation in Music.* New Haven: Yale Univ. Press, 1921.

Boring, Edwin G. *Sensation and Perception in the History of Experimental Psychology.* New York: Appleton-Century, 1942.

Chambers, G. B. *Folksong—Plainsong: A Study in Origins and Musical Relationships.* London: Merlin Press, 1956.

Cooper, Grosvenor W., and Leonard B. Meyer. *The Rhythmic Structure of Music.* Chicago: Univ. of Chicago Press, 1960.

Crocker, Richard L. "*Musica Rhythmica* and *Musica Metrica* in Antique and Medieval Theory." *Journal of Music Theory,* 2 (1958), 2–23.

Gajard, Dom Joseph. *The Rhythm of Plainsong.* Trans. Dom Aldhelm Dean. New York: J. Fischer, 1945.

———. *The Solesmes Method: Its Fundamental Principles and Rules of Interpretation.* Trans. R. Cecile Gabain. Collegeville, Minn.: Liturgical Press, 1960.

Gelineau, Joseph, S. J. *Voices and Instruments in Christian Worship.* Trans. Clifford Howell, S. J. Collegeville, Minn.: Liturgical Press, 1964.

Graduale Romanum. Paris, Tournai, Rome: Desclée & Socii, 1948.

Johner, Dom Dominic. *A New School of Gregorian Chant.* 3rd English ed. Ed. Herman Erpf and Max Ferrars. New York: Frederick Pustet, 1925.

Langer, Suzanne K. *Feeling and Form.* New York: Scribner's, 1953.

Le Guennant, A. *Préces de rythmique grégorienne d'après des principes de Solesmes.* Paris: by author, 6 rue Sainte-Beuve, 1952.

Luecke, Jane Marie. "Some Linguistic Criteria in the Accommodation of the English Mass Text to Sung Recitative and Melody." *Caecilia,* 91 (1964), 48–62.

———. "Adapting the Psalm Tones to English." *Liturgical Arts Quarterly,* 34 (1965), 7–12.

MacDougall, Robert. "The Structure of Simple Rhythm Forms." *Harvard Psychological Studies,* 1. Ed. Hugo Munsterberg. New York: Macmillan, 1903, 309–411.

Machlis, Joseph. *Introduction to Contemporary Music.* New York: Norton, 1961.

Mocquereau, Dom André. *Le Nombre musical grégorien: A Study of Gregorian Musical Rhythm.* Vol. 1, Part 1. Trans. Aileen Tone. Tournai: Desclée, 1932.

———. *Le Nombre musical grégorien.* Vol. 1, Part 2. Trans. Aileen Tone. Tournai: Desclée, 1951.

———. *Le Nombre musical grégorien ou rythmique grégorienne: Theorie et pratique.* Part 3. Tournai: Desclée, 1927.

New Oxford History of Music. Vol. I: *Ancient and Oriental Music.* Ed. Egon Wellesz (1957). Vol. II: *Early Medieval Music Up to 1300.* Ed. Anselm Hughes. London: Oxford Univ. Press, 1954.

Paléographie musicale: *Les Principaux manuscrits de chant grégorien, ambrosien, mozarabe, gallican, publiés en fac-similés phototypiques par les bénédictins de Solesmes.* 14 vols. Solesmes: Imprimerie Saint-Pierre, 1889–1931.

Palmer, Robert B. "Bede as Textbook Writer: A Study of His *De Arte Metrica.*" *Speculum,* 34 (1959), 573–84.

Pierik, Marie. *Dramatic and Symbolic Elements in Gregorian Chant.* New York: Desclee 1963.

———. *The Song of the Church.* New York: Longmans, Green, 1947.

Pothier, Dom Joseph. *Les Mélodies grégoriennes.* Tournai: Desclée Lefebvre, 1880.

Reese, Gustave. *Music in the Middle Ages with an Introduction on the Music of Ancient Times.* New York: Norton, 1940.

Ruckmich, Christian A. "The Role of Kinaesthesis in the Perception of Rhythm." *American Journal of Psychology,* 24 (1913), 305–59.

Sachs, Curt. *Rhythm and Tempo: A Study in Music History.* New York: Norton, 1953.

Smithers, Howard Elbert. "Theories of Rhythm in the Nineteenth and Twentieth Centuries With a Contribution to the Theory of Rhythm for the Study of Twentieth Century Music." Diss. Cornell 1960.

Sonnenschein, Edward Adolf. *What is Rhythm? An Essay.* Oxford: Basil Blackwell, 1925.

Stetson, Raymond B. "A Motor Theory of Rhythm and Discrete Sensation." *Psychological Review,* 12 (1905), 250–70, 293–350.

——. *Motor Phonetics: A Study of Speech Movements in Action.* 2nd ed. Amsterdam: North-Holland Publishing Company, 1951.

Suñol, Dom Gregory. *Text Book of Gregorian Chant According to the Solesmes Method.* Trans. (from 6th French ed.) G. M. Durnford. New York: J. Fischer, 1930.

Taig, Thomas. *Rhythm and Metre.* Cardiff: Univ. of Wales Press, 1929.

Twaddell, W. F. "Stetson's Model and the 'Supra-segmental Phonemes.'" *Language,* 29 (1953), 415–53.

Vollaerts, J. W. A. *Rhythmic Proportions in Early Medieval Ecclesiastical Chant.* Leiden: E. J. Brill, 1958.

Walker, D. P. "Some Aspects and Problems of *Musique mesurée à l'antique:* The Rhythm and Notation of Musique Mesurée." *Musica Disciplina,* 4 (1950), 163–86.

van Waesberghe, J. Smits. *Gregorian Chant.* Stockholm: Continental Book Company, n.d.

——. Review of *Rhythmic Proportions in Early Medieval Ecclesiastical Chant,* by J. W. A. Vollaerts. *Caecilia,* 87 (1960), 128–37.

Wagner, Peter. *Introduction to the Gregorian Melodies: A Handbook of Plainsong.* Part I. Trans. Agnes Orme and E. G. P. Wyatt. Rpt. in *Caecilia,* 84 (1957), 99–142, 201–36, 298–344; 85(1958), 51–102, 178–232, 279–320; 86(1959), 13–36. (Originally published for the Plainsong and Medieval Music Society, London.)

Westergaard, Peter. "Some Problems in Rhythmic Theory and Analysis." *Perspectives Of New Music,* 1 (1962), 180–91.

INDEX